Get More Clients
You Love:

Mastering the Alignment
Attraction Framework

Trish Saemann

Practical Wisdom Press
Charlotte, North Carolina

Practical Wisdom Press
TURNING WISDOM INTO WEALTH

Table of Contents

Acknowledgments

Writing a book is a journey that no author completes alone. This work exists because of the countless individuals who supported, inspired, and guided me along the way.

First and foremost, I want to thank my loving family for their unwavering support and patience throughout this process. Brian, you have always been my quiet champion, sweetest companion, and my unwavering best friend. Your encouragement kept me going during the long hours and late nights when the words wouldn't come easily. This book would not have seen the light of day without you.

To my editor, Jessica, whose keen eye and thoughtful suggestions transformed this manuscript from a rough draft into the polished work it is today. Your expertise and dedication to the craft have been invaluable.

Finally, to Carolina, Hannah, and Lindsey (see Chapter 10) who kept me grounded throughout this journey – who knew when to ask about the book's progress and when to talk about anything else – thank you. Your friendship means more than words can express.

And to you, the reader, thank you for choosing to spend your valuable time with these pages. I hope you find within them something meaningful to take with you.

With gratitude,

Trish

Introduction:
Why I Wrote This Book

I never imagined an ice cream cone could change my life, but sometimes, the universe has a way of serving up wake-up calls in the most unexpected flavors.

In late July, on a sun-drenched afternoon at a mini-golf course, the air was filled with the sound of laughter and the gentle clinking of putters against neon-colored golf balls. My youngest son, Connor, just seven years old, had just triumphantly completed his favorite activity. His face was alight with joy, the kind of pure happiness that only a child can radiate. It should have been a perfect moment, a memory to cherish.

Instead, I found myself standing in the parking lot, a good distance away from my family, my phone pressed tightly against my ear like it was surgically attached. On the other end was a client—not even my direct client, whose business we white-labeled for—and he was yelling. The words washed over me in an angry torrent, his pattern of awful behavior had become familiar by now. Too familiar.

As I stood there, trying to placate this man who seemed to own more of my time and mental energy than I did, I saw my family lining up for ice cream. Connor, in his exaggerated seven-year-old fashion, was waving at me. "Come on, Mom!" his gestures seemed to say. The gulf between where I stood and where I wanted to be felt immense, unbridgeable.

At that moment, something inside me snapped. It wasn't just about the interrupted vacation, though that was part of it. It wasn't even about this particular client, though his shouting was the immediate trigger. No, this was about all the moments I'd missed, all the times my business had taken precedence over my life. It was about realizing that I had somehow, without really noticing, given away control of my time, my energy, and my peace of mind.

With his outsized influence on my business, this client had become more than just a difficult partner. He had become a symbol of everything that was wrong with how I was running my company. I had allowed myself to become dependent on his business, and in doing so, I'd sacrificed my autonomy, my family time, and my joy.

As I watched, Connor's waving become more insistent, I made a promise to myself. This had to change. I needed to find a way to attract the kind of clients I wanted to work with—clients who valued my expertise respected my time and aligned with my vision. I needed to reshape my business so that it served my life, not the other way around.

That's why I wrote this book.

This book was born from that moment in the parking lot, from the realization that too many of us in the business world find ourselves trapped in cycles of frustration, working with clients who drain our energy rather than inspire our best work. It's for every entrepreneur who's ever felt owned by their clients instead of empowered by them. It's for every business owner who's missed a family moment because they were putting out fires for a client who didn't truly value their work.

In the pages that follow, I'll share the journey I embarked on after that day. I'll show you how I transformed my approach to marketing, and how I learned to attract aligned clients who energized rather than exhausted me. You'll learn the strategies I developed to build a business that supports my life goals instead of hindering them.

But more than that, this book is a call to action. I want to help and implore you to reclaim your business and your life. It's about understanding that you have the power to choose your clients, set the terms of your engagements, and build a business that brings you joy as well as profit.

As I write this, I'm happy to report that I've fully enjoyed and participated in many more family outings since that day at the mini-golf course. I've enjoyed ice cream with my kids without interruption. I've built a client base that respects my boundaries and values my contributions. I've transformed my business into one that allows me to be present for the moments that matter most.

I hope that this book will help you do the same. Whether you're just starting out or you've been in business for years, whether you're feeling trapped by difficult clients, or you're ready to take your business to the next level, this book is for you.

So, let's begin this journey together. Let's explore how you can attract the right clients, build the right relationships, and create a business that serves your life in all the ways that matter most. Because at the end of the day, that's what true success looks like—a thriving business that allows you to be there, fully present, for all of life's precious moments, big and small.

Transforming Your Business
with the Alignment Attraction Framework

Welcome to *Get More Clients You Love: Mastering the Alignment Attraction Framework.* You're about to embark on a transformative journey that will revolutionize how you attract clients and run your business. If you've ever found yourself working with clients who drain your energy, undervalue your services, or simply don't align with your vision, this book is your roadmap to change.

How cool would it be if every client interaction energized you? Your work would feel purposeful and appreciated, and your growth would be fueled by genuine connections with clients who truly value what you offer. This isn't a pipe dream, but I used to think it was—it's the reality that the Alignment Attraction Framework can help you create.

At its core, the Alignment Attraction Framework is about more than just getting more clients. It's about attracting the right clients—those who resonate with your unique approach, appreciate your value, and bring out the best in your work. This framework integrates seamlessly with the proven "Get More Clients You Love" method, enhancing each of the nine Ms: Mindset, Mission, Market, Message, Medium, Money, Measure, Mechanism, and Maintain. I've added a bonus "M" to the framework that was not included when I first created this methodology but certainly should have been. The Bonus "M" has had the most profound impact on my life, both personally and professionally.

As you read this book, you'll discover:

1. How to define and deeply understand your ideal client, going beyond surface-level demographics to uncover the true essence of who you serve best.

2. Techniques to craft a compelling message that speaks directly to your ideal clients' hearts and minds, naturally attracting them to your services.

3. Strategies for positioning yourself in the market as the go-to expert for your specific niche, making you the obvious choice for your ideal clients.

4. Methods to leverage the right channels and create content that not only reaches your ideal clients but also pre-qualifies them.

5. Approaches to pricing and packaging your services in a way that reflects your true value and attracts high-quality clients.

6. Systems and processes to support exceptional client relationships from the first point of contact through long-term engagement.

7. Techniques for confidently handling objections and gracefully turning clients who are a poor ensuring every interaction aligns with your business values.

This book is not about quick fixes or manipulative tactics. It's about creating deep, authentic alignment between who you are, what you offer, and the clients you serve. It's about building a sustainable, fulfilling business that not only provides financial success but also personal satisfaction.

Whether you're just starting your entrepreneurial journey or you're a seasoned business owner looking to elevate your client base, the Alignment Attraction Framework will provide you with powerful tools and insights to transform your approach to client attraction and retention.

As we progress through each section, you'll be guided through practical exercises and real-world examples that will help you apply the framework to your unique business. By the end of this book, you'll have a clear roadmap for attracting more clients you love and building a business that truly reflects your values and vision.

So, are you ready to say goodbye to client frustrations and hello to a business filled with ideal clients who energize and inspire you? Let's begin this exciting journey of transformation with the Alignment Attraction Framework. Your journey toward working with clients you love starts now!

Chapter 1:
Mindset — Cultivating the Entrepreneur's Magnetic Mindset

―――――――――――――――――

Identifying and Overcoming Limiting Beliefs About Client Relationships

As entrepreneurs, we often carry hidden baggage that weighs us down on our journey to success. These sneaky saboteurs are our limiting beliefs about client relationships, which are like invisible chains holding us back from the thriving business we deserve.

Picture this: You're sitting at your desk, staring at your phone, heart racing as you prepare to call a potential client. But a tiny voice in your head whispers, *They'll probably think my prices are too high.* Sound familiar? That's a limiting belief in action, and it's time to kick them all to the curb.

The first step in overcoming these pesky thought patterns is to shine a spotlight on them. Grab a journal and jot down every negative thought that crosses your mind when you think about client interactions. Don't hold back—do a brain dump. You might be surprised at what's been lurking in the shadows of your mind.

Now, let's play detective. For each limiting belief you've uncovered, ask yourself: *Is this really true? Where did this belief come from?* Maybe you had a bad experience with a client in the past, or perhaps you're echoing something a well-meaning but misguided mentor once told you. Understanding the root of these beliefs is like finding the source of a river—once you know where it starts, you can change its course.

It's time to flip the script. For every limiting belief, we're going to create an empowering alternative. To combat the little voice that says, *They'll think your prices are too high.* Replace it with, *My prices reflect the value I provide, and the right clients will appreciate that.* Feel the difference? It's like switching from a cramped economy seat to first class—suddenly, there's room to breathe and grow.

But identifying and reframing these beliefs is just the beginning. The real magic happens when you put your new, empowering thoughts into action. The next time you're about to reach out to a potential client, pause for a moment. Take a deep breath and remind yourself of your new empowering belief. Let it sink in and guide your actions.

Rewiring your brain takes time and practice. Be patient with yourself as you navigate this process towards change. Celebrate the small victories—every time you catch yourself in a limiting belief and choose to reframe it, you're one step closer to attracting the high-quality clients you deserve.

By consistently challenging and overcoming your limiting beliefs about client relationships, you're not just changing your thoughts—you're transforming your entire business ecosystem. You're creating a magnetic mindset that naturally attracts ideal clients who value your work and respect your worth. And that, my friend, is the foundation of a business you'll truly love.

Developing an Abundance Mentality for Attracting Ideal Clients

An abundance mentality is like a magical watering can for your business. It's the belief that there are more than enough ideal clients out there for everyone, including you. When you embrace this mindset, you stop seeing other entrepreneurs as the competition and start viewing them as potential collaborators in a vast, ever-expanding market.

But right now, you might be focused on tending to a barren patch of land, desperately trying to make something grow in dry, cracked soil. It's time to change that landscape and cultivate an oasis of opportunity.

So how do you start cultivating this abundance mentality? It begins with a simple shift in perspective. Instead of thinking, *I hope I can find a client this month*, try, *There are countless ideal clients out there eagerly searching for exactly what I offer*. Feel the difference? It's like switching from a flickering candle to a blazing bonfire of possibilities.

Now, let's get practical. Start each day by visualizing a world brimming with perfect clients for your business. See them lined up at your door, inbox overflowing with inquiries, phone ringing off the hook. Really feel the excitement and gratitude of having more opportunities than you can handle. This isn't just daydreaming—it's programming your brain to spot and seize abundant opportunities.

Next, it's time to put on your scientist hat and gather evidence. Keep a daily "Abundance Log" where you jot down every instance of abundance you witness in your life and business. Did a colleague land a big contract? Celebrate it as proof of the plentiful opportunities out there. Did you overhear someone expressing their need for exactly the kind of service you provide? Another point for abundance!

As you train your brain to spot abundance, you'll notice a snowball effect. The more evidence you gather, the stronger your abundance mentality grows. It's like tuning a radio to pick up a specific frequency—suddenly, you're hearing opportunities loud and clear that you might have missed before.

But abundance isn't just about what you can get—it's also about what you can give. Look for ways to add value to your network without expecting immediate returns. Share helpful resources, make introductions, offer genuine compliments. This generosity isn't just good karma—it positions you as a valuable node in your professional network, attracting even more opportunities your way.

Developing an abundance mentality is a journey, not a destination. There will be days when scarcity thoughts try to creep back in. When that happens, pause and gently remind yourself of all the evidence you've gathered in your Abundance Log. Let it wash over you like a refreshing shower, rinsing away those scarcity cobwebs.

As your abundance mentality flourishes, you'll notice a remarkable shift in your client attraction efforts. You'll approach prospects with genuine confidence, knowing that whether this particular opportunity works out or not, there are plenty more on the horizon. This relaxed, assured energy is irresistibly attractive to high-quality clients who are looking for a partner, not just a service provider.

Embrace the abundance mindset and watch as your business transforms from a parched patch of land into a flourishing oasis, attracting ideal clients like bees to a field of blooming flowers. The garden of your dreams is within reach—you just need to believe in its possibilities and nurture it with your newfound abundance mentality.

Cultivating Self-Worth and Its Impact on Client Attraction

Self-worth is the secret ingredient that transforms your business from a shy wallflower to the belle of the ball. It's not about ego or arrogance—it's about recognizing and owning the true value you bring to the table. When you deeply believe in your worth, it radiates from you like a beacon, attracting high-quality clients who resonate with your confidence and expertise.

But let's face it—cultivating self-worth isn't always a walk in the park. Many of us have picked up some nasty habits along the way, like downplaying our achievements or constantly comparing ourselves to others. It's time to break free from these self-sabotaging patterns and step into your full potential.

Start by taking stock of your unique blend of skills, experiences, and qualities. What makes you, well, you? Maybe it's your knack for simplifying complex problems, your infectious enthusiasm, or your ability to see connections others miss. Write these down—not as a brag list, but as a factual inventory of your professional assets. This isn't the time for modesty—be honest about what you bring to the table.

Now, let's tackle the comparison trap. Every time you catch yourself measuring your progress against someone else's highlight reel, pause. Remind yourself that you're seeing their carefully curated public image, not their behind-the-scenes struggles. Instead of comparing, get curious. What can you learn from their success? How can it inspire you to level up in your own unique way?

Another powerful tool for cultivating self-worth is to keep a "Victory File." This is a collection of positive feedback, successful project outcomes, and personal wins. On days when your self-worth feels shaky, dive into this file. Let it remind you of the value you've consistently delivered and the lives you've positively impacted through your work.

But self-worth isn't just about past achievements—it's also about how you treat yourself in the present. Start paying attention to your self-talk. Would you speak to a dear friend the way you speak to yourself?

If not, it's time for a language makeover. Replace harsh self-criticism with kind, encouraging words. It might feel awkward at first but stick with it. You're reprogramming years of habitual thinking.

As your self-worth grows, you'll notice a shift in how you interact with potential clients. Instead of desperately trying to prove your value, you'll approach conversations with calm confidence. You'll be able to clearly articulate your worth without feeling boastful or apologetic. This authentic confidence acts like a magnet for attracting high-quality clients who are looking for a true partner, not just a service provider.

Remember, cultivating self-worth is an ongoing process. There will be days when you feel on top of the world, and others when doubts creep in. That's normal. The key is to have tools and practices in place to nurture your self-worth consistently.

As you continue to strengthen your sense of self-worth, you'll find that client attraction becomes almost effortless. You'll naturally repel clients who undervalue your services and attract those who appreciate your true worth. Your business will evolve from constantly chasing after any client to confidently welcoming ideal partnerships.

So, stand tall at your marketplace stall. Let your self-worth shine through in every interaction, every proposal, every piece of work you deliver. The right clients—the ones who will truly value you—will be drawn to your light like moths to a flame. Your journey to attracting high-quality clients begins with recognizing and owning your innate worth. Embrace it, nurture it, and watch your business flourish.

Aligning Personal Values with Business Goals

Many entrepreneurs set their business goals without ever taking a deep dive into their personal values. It's like setting sail without checking your compass. You might make progress, but are you heading in the right direction? When your business goals align with these core values, you're not just moving forward—you're charting a course to your truest, most fulfilling destination.

First things first—let's uncover your personal values. Grab a warm drink, settle into a cozy spot, and let's do some soul-searching. What matters most to you in life? Is it creativity, integrity, freedom, growth, or perhaps making a positive impact? Don't rush this process. Sit with each value, feel its importance in your gut. These aren't just words—they're the bedrock of who you are and how you want to show up in the world.

Once you've identified your core values, it's time to play detective with your current business goals. Think about your mission statement, consider your day to day business, are you spending your time in ways that align with your personal values? It's okay if you notice some misalignment—that's valuable information. It's like realizing you've been wearing shoes that are a size too small. No wonder you've felt uncomfortable about your professional goals.

Now comes the exciting part—realigning your business goals to dance in harmony with your personal values. If freedom is a core value, how can you structure your business to give you more autonomy? If creativity tops your list, are your goals nurturing that spark or smothering it under piles of mundane tasks? This isn't about throwing out all your existing goals—it's about refining and reshaping them to reflect what truly matters to you.

As you align your goals with your values, you might notice some resistance. Maybe that revenue target feels at odds with your value of work-life balance. Don't shy away from these tensions—they're opportunities for creative problem-solving. How can you hit that financial goal while still honoring your need for personal time? Perhaps it's about working smarter, not harder, or pivoting to higher-value services that allow you to earn more in less time.

Here's where the magic happens: as your business goals come into alignment with your personal values, you'll start attracting clients who share those values. It's like tuning a radio to pick up a specific frequency—suddenly, you're hearing opportunities loud and clear that you might have missed before. Clients who appreciate your commitment to creativity, integrity, or whatever your core values may be, will naturally gravitate towards you.

This alignment creates a beautiful authenticity in your business that is irresistible to high-quality clients. When your marketing messages, service offerings, and client interactions all stem from your core values, you create a consistent, genuine brand that stands out in a sea of hollow promises and flashy gimmicks.

Creating alignment is not a one-and-done deal. As you grow and develop, so might your values and goals. Make it a habit to check in regularly. Are your business practices still in sync with what matters most to you? This ongoing reflection keeps your business agile and authentic, so you are ready to pivot when needed while staying true to your core.

By aligning your personal values with your business goals, you're not just building a successful enterprise—you're crafting a legacy that reflects your truest self. You're creating a business that energizes you, attracts ideal clients, and makes a meaningful impact in the way only you can.

So, captain of your entrepreneurial ship, are you ready to align your compass and chart a course to true fulfillment? Your values are the wind in your sails, propelling you toward a horizon of success that's uniquely, wonderfully yours. Set your course and watch as the right opportunities and ideal clients appear on your journey, drawn to the authentic beacon of your aligned business.

Chapter 2:
Mission — Aligning Your Business Purpose with Client Attraction

Defining Your Company's Mission:
The North Star of Your Business

As small business owners, we often find ourselves caught in the whirlwind of daily operations. We're juggling financial management, client services, team leadership, and a myriad of other tasks. In this constant flurry of activity, it's alarmingly easy to lose sight of why we embarked on this journey in the first place. This is where defining your company's mission becomes not just important, but crucial.

Think of your mission as the heartbeat of your company. It's not a mere sentence to be framed and forgotten on an office wall. Rather, it's the very essence of why your business exists. It's the purpose that gets you out of bed every morning, eager to make a difference in the world through your work.

When you take the time to reflect on and articulate your mission, you're giving yourself and your team a clear sense of purpose. It's like having a compass that always points true north, especially valuable when you're faced with tough decisions or navigating uncertain times. Your mission becomes the litmus test for every opportunity, every strategy, every client you consider working with.

But how do you define this mission? Start by asking yourself some deep, probing questions:

- Why did I start this business in the first place?

- What problem am I solving in the world?

- What impact do I want to have on my clients and community?

- What legacy do I want to leave through my work?

The answers to these questions will help you distill the core purpose of your business. A powerful mission statement isn't about what you do, but why you do it. It's not about the services you offer, but the transformation you create.

As you craft your mission statement, keep it clear, concise, and inspiring. It should be easy to understand and remember, yet profound enough to stir emotions and drive action. A well-crafted mission statement should resonate not just with you, but with your team, your clients, and your broader community.

Defining your mission isn't a one-time task. As your business grows and changes, revisit your mission regularly. Does it still align with your values and goals? Does it still inspire and guide you? Be open to refining and evolving your mission as your business journey unfolds.

By taking the time to define and articulate your company's mission, you're not just creating a statement—you're setting the foundation for a business that's deeply aligned with your values and purpose. This alignment becomes a powerful force in attracting the right clients, the right team members, and the right opportunities. It's the first step in creating a business that not only succeeds financially but also fulfills you on a deeper, more meaningful level.

Leveraging Your Mission to Attract Aligned Clients

Your mission statement functions like a powerful magnet, drawing in not just any clients, but attracting the ones who resonate deeply with your purpose and values. When you clearly articulate and embody your mission, you create a magnetic field that naturally attracts clients who share your vision and appreciate the unique value you bring to the table.

But how exactly does your mission statement become a client attraction tool? It starts with infusing your mission into every aspect of your business. Your mission shouldn't be a hidden gem, tucked away in a forgotten document. It should be the beating heart of your brand, pulsing through every interaction, every piece of content, every service you offer.

Begin by prominently featuring your mission on your website, not as a dull corporate statement, but as a compelling story that invites potential clients into your world. Share the "why" behind your business—what drove you to start this journey, what impact you're striving to make. This vulnerability and authenticity create an emotional connection with potential clients who share similar values and aspirations.

Next, weave your mission into your marketing messages. Instead of focusing solely on the features of your services, highlight how your work aligns with your mission and the broader impact it creates. For example, if your mission revolves around empowering small businesses to thrive, don't just talk about your accounting services. Paint a picture of how your work contributes to the success and growth of local economies.

Your mission can also guide your content creation strategy. Develop blog posts, videos, or podcasts that not only showcase your expertise but also reflect your mission and values. This approach attracts clients who are looking for more than just a service provider—they're seeking a partner who shares their worldview and is committed to making a difference.

When it comes to networking and partnerships, let your mission be your guide. Seek out events, collaborations, and partnerships that align with your purpose. This not only puts you in front of potential clients who share your values but also surrounds you with a community that reinforces and amplifies your mission.

Clients today, especially high-value clients, are often looking for more than just a transactional relationship. They want to work with businesses that stand for something and have a purpose beyond profit. By clearly communicating and living your mission, you position yourself as a purpose-driven business, which can be a powerful differentiator in a crowded market.

Your mission can also help in pre-qualifying potential clients. When you're clear about your purpose and values, it naturally filters out clients who aren't aligned with your vision. This saves you time and energy, ensuring that you focus on building relationships with clients who truly appreciate and resonate with what you offer.

As you leverage your mission to attract clients, be prepared for deeper, more meaningful client relationships. Clients who are drawn to your mission are more likely to be invested in long-term partnerships, to be advocates for your brand, and to derive greater satisfaction from working with you.

Lastly, don't underestimate the power of your mission to inspire referrals. Clients who feel connected to your purpose are more likely to share their experience with others who share similar values. Your mission becomes a story they want to be part of and share with others.

By leveraging your mission to attract aligned clients, you're not just filling your client roster—you're building a community of like-minded individuals who believe in what you do and why you do it. This alignment creates a virtuous cycle, where your work becomes more fulfilling, your impact grows, and your business naturally attracts more of the clients you love to serve.

Aligning Your Team with Your Mission for Cohesive Client Experiences

Team alignment is the cornerstone of working in "concert." Every team member is a vital instrument, and when they're all in tune with your mission, the result is a harmonious and powerful performance that captivates your ideal clients. This is the transformative power of aligning your team with your mission. It makes for KILLER customer service reviews too.

First, let's acknowledge a fundamental truth: your mission is only as powerful as your team's embodiment of it. It's not enough for your mission to be a well-crafted statement—it needs to be a living, breathing force that guides every action and decision in your business. And this starts with your team.

Begin by making your mission a central part of your hiring process. When interviewing potential team members, don't just focus on skills and experience. Dive deep into their values, their aspirations, and their own sense of purpose. Ask questions that reveal whether their personal mission aligns with your company's mission. Remember, skills can be taught, but alignment of values and purpose is fundamental.

Once you have a team in place, make your mission a cornerstone of your onboarding process. Don't just hand new team members a manual with the mission statement printed on the first page. Instead, create immersive experiences that bring your mission to life. This could be through storytelling sessions where you and long-time team members share stories of how the mission has guided decisions and impacted clients. Or it could be through hands-on projects that immediately connect new hires with the purpose of your work.

Regular team meetings are another powerful opportunity to reinforce your mission. Start meetings by revisiting your mission and sharing recent examples of how it's been put into action. Encourage team members to share their own stories of how they've seen the mission come to life in their work. This not only keeps the mission front and center but also helps team members see the direct impact of their work.

Create a culture where decisions at all levels are filtered through the lens of your mission. Empower your team members to ask, "Does this align with our mission?" when faced with choices or challenges. This not only ensures consistency in your business practices but also gives team members a sense of ownership and purpose in their roles.

Recognition and rewards are powerful tools for reinforcing mission alignment. When acknowledging great work, don't just focus on results—highlight how the work exemplified your mission. Create awards or recognition programs that specifically celebrate mission-aligned actions and decisions.

Your team members are the primary point of contact for many of your clients. When they're deeply aligned with your mission, this shines through in every interaction. Clients don't just experience KILLER service; they feel the purpose and passion behind your work. This creates a cohesive, powerful client experience that sets you apart from competitors who may offer similar services but lack a unifying mission.

Encourage your team to personalize the mission. While the overall company mission remains constant, allow team members to articulate how this mission translates into their specific roles. This personal connection deepens their commitment and allows them to communicate the mission more authentically to clients.

Be open to input from your team on how to better live out your mission. They're on the front lines, interacting with clients and implementing your services. They may have valuable insights on how to more fully embody your mission or even ways the mission might evolve as your business grows.

Lastly, lead by example. As the business owner, you are the primary ambassador of your mission. Your team will follow and come to depend on your example to see how the mission translates into day-to-day actions and decisions. When you consistently embody your mission, it inspires and empowers your team to do the same.

By aligning your team with your mission, you create a powerful, unified force that attracts and serves your ideal clients. This alignment transforms your business from a group of individuals performing tasks to a cohesive team driven by a shared purpose. The result is not just satisfied clients, but true advocates who are drawn to the authentic, mission-driven experience your business provides. In this way, your mission becomes more than words—it becomes the very essence of your business, felt, and appreciated by every client you serve.

Evolving Your Mission as Your Business Grows

As entrepreneurs, we often craft our initial mission statements when our businesses are in their infancy. We have dreams, aspirations, and a general sense of the impact we want to make. But as we gain experience, as we interact with more clients, and as we face the realities and opportunities of our market, our understanding of our purpose often deepens and broadens.

The key to updating your mission is to stay attuned to both your internal growth and the changing needs of your clients and community. Set regular intervals—perhaps annually or bi-annually—to reflect deeply on your mission. Ask yourself and your team:

- Does our current mission still ignite passion and drive our best work?

- Has our understanding of our impact and the problems we solve deepened?

- Are there new aspects of our work that our mission doesn't fully capture?

- How have our clients' needs, and the market landscape changed?

- Does our mission still differentiate us in a meaningful way?

This reflection process isn't about discarding your original mission, but about allowing it to mature. Think of it as refining a rough diamond— you're not changing its essential nature but revealing more of its inherent brilliance and facets.

As you consider evolving your mission, involve your team and even your long-term clients in the process. They can provide valuable perspectives on how your business has impacted them and what they see as your unique value proposition. This collaborative approach not only leads to a more robust mission but also increases buy-in and alignment across your stakeholders.

When you do make changes to your mission, communicate them clearly and enthusiastically. Share the reasoning behind the evolution, connecting it to the growth and successes you've experienced. This transparency helps maintain trust and excitement among your team and clients.

Revising and growing your mission isn't about following trends or trying to be all things to all people. It's about staying true to your core purpose while allowing it to expand and deepen. A well-evolved mission maintains the essence of why you started your business while reflecting the greater impact and more nuanced understanding you've developed over time.

As your mission evolves, make sure this growth is reflected in all aspects of your business. Update your marketing materials, revisit your service offerings, and possibly even reconsider your target market. An evolved mission might open doors to new opportunities or client segments that align more closely with your expanded vision.

Be prepared for the possibility that some team members or clients might not resonate with your expanded mission. While this can be challenging, it's also an opportunity to reaffirm who you are as a business and to attract team members and clients who are even more aligned with your deepened purpose.

Transforming your mission can also be a powerful tool for reinvigorating your business. It can breathe new life into your work, inspiring fresh creativity, and renewed passion. This energy is contagious—it excites your team, attracts new clients, and can open doors to unexpected opportunities.

As you go through this evolution, stay connected to your original inspiration. Your initial mission came from a place of genuine passion and purpose. Your evolved mission should build on this foundation, honoring your roots while reaching toward new heights.

The goal of advancing your mission is not to create a perfect, unchanging statement. It's about ensuring that your mission remains a vivid, accurate reflection of why your business exists and the unique value it brings to the world. By allowing your mission to grow and evolve, you ensure that it continues to be a powerful force in attracting aligned clients, inspiring your team, and driving your business towards ever-greater impact and success.

Chapter 3:
Market — Defining
and Attracting Your Dream Client Avatar

Creating a Detailed Ideal Client Profile
Using the Alignment Attraction Framework

If you could walk into a room full of potential clients and instantly spot the ones who are perfect for your business—the ones who light up when they hear about your services, who value your expertise, and who you'd be thrilled to work with, how impactful would that be to your bottom line and peace of mind? That's the power of creating a detailed ideal client profile using the Alignment Attraction Framework.

Let's roll up our sleeves and dive into this transformative process. First, we need to shift our mindset. Instead of casting a wide net and hoping to catch any client, we're going to focus on attracting the cream of the crop. Think quality over quantity. This approach might feel counterintuitive at first, like you're limiting your options. But trust me, when you target the right clients, your business will thrive in ways you never imagined.

Start by reflecting on your past client experiences. Who were the clients that made you jump out of bed excited to work? Think about the ones where the projects flowed smoothly, communication was a breeze, and the results were stellar. Jot down what made these experiences so positive. Was it their communication style? Their values? Their approach to your work?

Now, let's flip the coin. Think about the clients who drained your energy, the ones who had you checking the clock every five minutes. What were the red flags you missed? This exercise isn't about dwelling on negative experiences, but about learning from them to refine your ideal client profile.

With these insights in mind, it's time to breathe life into your ideal client avatar. Give them a name, a face, a personality. What kind of car do they drive? What keeps them up at night? What are their biggest dreams and deepest fears? The more vivid and detailed you make this avatar, the easier it will be to spot your ideal clients in the real world.

But here's where the Alignment Attraction Framework takes things to the next level. Instead of just focusing on demographics or surface-level characteristics, we're going to dig deeper. What are the core values that drive your ideal client? How do these align with your own values and the mission of your business? This alignment is the secret sauce that creates those dream client relationships.

Consider their communication style, decision-making process, and how they measure success. Do they prefer quick, to-the-point exchanges or in-depth discussions? Are they data-driven or more intuitive in their choices? Understanding these nuances will help you tailor your approach and create instant rapport with your ideal clients.

Don't forget to consider their pain points and aspirations. What problems are they desperately trying to solve? What goals are they striving to achieve? Your services should be the bridge that helps them cross from their current struggles to their desired outcomes.

As you flesh out this profile, you might worry that you're being too specific, that your ideal client doesn't exist in the real world. But here's the beautiful truth—by creating this detailed avatar, you're tuning your business to a specific frequency. And when you broadcast on that frequency, you'll be amazed at how many ideal clients start to appear, as if by magic.

Over time, as your business grows and changes and you gain new insights, don't be afraid to refine and adjust your avatar. It's a living, breathing touchstone that grows with you and your business.

By creating this detailed ideal client profile using the Alignment Attraction Framework, you're not just defining who you want to work with—you're setting the stage for transformative client relationships that will elevate your business to new heights. Get ready to attract clients who not only appreciate your work but who inspire you to do your best work. This is where creating your own business becomes a true joy, and success follows naturally.

Identifying Pain Points and Desires of Your Target Market

Understanding your ideal clients' pain points is like finding the key to a locked treasure chest. These are the problems that keep your clients tossing and turning at night, the challenges that make their palms sweat and their hearts race. They're not just minor inconveniences—they're the big, hairy issues that your clients desperately want to solve.

To uncover these pain points, you need to become a detective. Start by listening—really listening—to your target market. Scour online forums, social media groups, and industry publications where your ideal clients hang out. What complaints come up again and again? What frustrations do they vent about? These recurring themes are gold mines of insight into your target market's pain points.

But don't stop at online sleuthing. Reach out directly to your ideal clients or those who fit your target profile. Conduct interviews or surveys. Ask open-ended questions that encourage them to share their struggles. "What's the biggest challenge you're facing in your business right now?" "If you had a magic wand, what problem would you solve instantly?" Asking questions like these can reveal pain points you might never have considered.

As you gather this information, patterns will emerge. Maybe you'll discover that your target market is struggling with time management, or perhaps they're grappling with how to stand out in a crowded market. Whatever their pain points are, write them down. They're the targets you'll be Aiming at when you're designing your services to solve their pain points.

Now, let's flip the coin and look at desires. If pain points are what your clients want to move away from, desires are what they want to move towards. These are the dreams, the aspirations, the "if only I could" wishes that motivate your ideal clients.

To uncover these desires, listen for the language of aspiration. What goals do your ideal clients talk about achieving? What do they envy in their more successful peers? What results do they dream of creating in their own lives or businesses?

Again, direct conversation is invaluable here. Ask questions like, "Where do you see yourself (or your business) in five years?" or "What would a perfect day look like for you?" Their answers will paint a vivid picture of your target market's desires.

As you explore both pain points and desires, look for the emotional undercurrents. Sure, a client might say they want to increase their revenue by 30 percent, but what's really driving that goal? Is it the desire for financial security? The dream of finally taking that luxury vacation? The hope of proving their doubters wrong? Understanding these emotional drivers will allow you to connect with your ideal clients on a deeper level.

Now, here's where the magic happens. Take all this rich information about pain points and desires and map it against your services or products. How does what you offer solve those pressing pain points? How does it help your clients achieve their deepest desires? This alignment is the sweet spot where your business can truly thrive.

Markets advance, new challenges arise, and desires shift. Make it a habit to regularly check in with your target market, to stay tuned into to their changing needs and wants.

By deeply understanding both the pain points and desires of your target market, you're no longer shooting blindfolded into the mist. You're a skilled archer with a clear target, able to aim your services with precision and impact. This understanding will inform everything from your marketing messages to your product development, ensuring that every aspect of your business resonates powerfully with your ideal clients.

Researching and Understanding Your Ideal Client's Decision-Making Process

What do all of your current, potential, and past clients have in common? They're human. To that end, we must acknowledge that decision-making isn't always logical. It's a complex dance of rational thought, emotional impulses, and subconscious biases. Your job is to become an expert in this dance; to understand the steps your ideal clients take from the moment they realize they have a need to the instant they decide to work with you.

Begin by mapping out the typical journey of your ideal client. Where do they usually start? Is it a sudden realization of a problem, a gradual awareness of a need, or perhaps a trigger event that sets them on the path to seeking your services? Understanding this starting point is crucial—it's where you need to position yourself to capture their attention.

Next, dive into their information-gathering phase. Where do your ideal clients go to learn more about their problems and potential solutions? Are they Google searchers, voracious blog readers, podcast listeners, or do they prefer to ask for recommendations from their network? This knowledge will help you plant your flag in the right territories, ensuring you're visible when your ideal clients are actively seeking answers.

But here's where many entrepreneurs miss a trick—they focus solely on the logical, surface-level aspects of decision-making. To truly understand your ideal clients, you need to delve deeper into the emotional and psychological factors at play. What fears might be holding them back from making a decision? What aspirations are driving them forward? Understanding these emotional undercurrents will allow you to address not just their logical needs, but their emotional ones too.

Consider the role of social proof in your ideal client's decision-making process. Do they place high value on testimonials and case studies? Are they influenced by industry awards or certifications? Or perhaps they're more swayed by personal recommendations from trusted peers? This insight will help you prioritize the types of social proof you showcase in your marketing efforts.

Another crucial aspect to explore is your ideal client's risk tolerance. Are they early adopters, eager to try new solutions? Or are they more cautious, needing extensive reassurance before making a decision? This understanding will inform how you present your offerings and the types of guarantees or risk-reducers you might need to provide.

Don't forget to investigate the timeline of their decision-making process. Are your ideal clients typically making quick, impulse decisions, or do they have a long, considered approach? This knowledge will help you tailor your follow-up strategy and sales process to match their pace, avoiding the pitfall of pushing too hard too soon or letting promising leads go cold.

As you gather these insights, look for patterns and commonalities. But also, be alert for variations. You might discover that your ideal clients fall into a few distinct categories, each with its own unique decision-making process. This nuanced understanding allows you to create tailored approaches for each segment.

Though it can feel this way at times, this research isn't about manipulation or trickery. It's about deeply understanding your ideal clients so you can serve them better. When you truly get how they make decisions, you can provide the right information, in the right format, at the right time. You're not just selling a service; you're guiding them through a journey, addressing their needs and concerns at every step.

By becoming an expert in your ideal client's decision-making process, you're equipping yourself with a powerful tool. You'll be able to create marketing messages that resonate, sales processes that feel natural and helpful, and client experiences that delight. This deep understanding is the difference between shouting into the void and having a meaningful conversation with your ideal clients. So, intrepid explorer, are you ready to uncover the secrets of your ideal client's decision-making process? The insights you gain will be worth their weight in gold.

Positioning Yourself in the Market to Attract High-Quality Clients

How do you make sure your ideal clients not only notice you but are magnetically drawn to what you offer? It's a question as old as capitalism itself. Learning and mastering the art of positioning is your ticket to attracting high-quality clients who value your unique gifts.

So what is positioning, exactly? Positioning isn't about shouting the loudest or having the flashiest display. It's about occupying a distinct, meaningful place in your ideal client's mind. Think of it as finding your perfect spot in a bustling marketplace—the place where your ideal clients naturally gravitate, where your offerings shine brightest.

To start, take a good, hard look at your strengths. What do you do better than anyone else? What unique combination of skills, experiences, and qualities do you bring to the table? This isn't the time for modesty—dig deep and own what makes you exceptional. Maybe it's your innovative approach, your unparalleled expertise in a niche area, or your ability to explain complex concepts with clarity and wit.

Now, consider your ideal clients. What do they value most? What problems keep them up at night? Your positioning sweet spot lies at the intersection of your unique strengths and your ideal clients' most pressing needs and deepest desires. This is where you plant your flag.

But here's the kicker—strong positioning often requires the courage to narrow your focus. It might feel counterintuitive, like you're limiting your potential client base. But remember, when you try to appeal to everyone, you end up truly resonating with no one. By positioning yourself as the go-to expert for a specific type of client or problem, you become the obvious choice for those who fit the bill.

Let's say you're a business coach. Instead of positioning yourself as a general coach who can help anyone with anything, you might focus on being the premier coach for introverted entrepreneurs looking to build sustainable six-figure businesses without burning out. Suddenly, you're not just another coach in the sea of sameness—you're a beacon for a specific group of ideal clients.

Once you've identified your positioning, it's time to weave it into every aspect of your business. Your website, your social media presence, your networking pitch—they should all clearly communicate your unique position. Use language that resonates with your ideal clients, addressing their specific pain points and aspirations. Show them that you understand their world and that you're uniquely equipped to help them navigate it.

But positioning isn't just about what you say—it's also about what you do. Every interaction with potential clients is an opportunity to reinforce your position. Deliver content that showcases your unique perspective. Offer services that align perfectly with your positioning. Even the way you structure your client onboarding process should reflect your distinct approach.

Strong positioning often means saying no to opportunities that don't align with your focus. This can be tough, especially when you're just starting out or going through a lean period. But each time you say no to a misaligned opportunity, you're saying a bigger yes to attracting your ideal, high-quality clients.

Don't be afraid to stand out from the crowd. In fact, if your positioning doesn't make some people scratch their heads, you might not be differentiating yourself enough. Your goal isn't to appeal to the masses— it's to be irresistible to your specific slice of the market.

Lastly, remember that positioning isn't a set-it-and-forget-it task. As your business evolves, as you gain new skills and insights, and as your market changes, your positioning may need to shift too. Stay tuned to your ideal clients' changing needs and be ready to adjust your position to stay relevant and compelling.

By thoughtfully positioning yourself in the market, you're not just another vendor in the crowded business marketplace. You become a beacon, drawing your ideal clients to you with the magnetic pull of perfect alignment. You'll find yourself attracting not just any clients, but high-quality clients who truly value what you offer, who are excited to work with you, and who bring out the best in your business. This is how you transform your business from a constant struggle for attention into a thriving hub for ideal client relationships.

Chapter 4:
Message — Crafting Your Irresistible Unique Selling Proposition (USP)

Developing a Compelling USP That Resonates with Your Ideal Clients

Your USP is not just a catchy tagline or a clever marketing gimmick. It's what makes your business distinct and distills that distinction into a clear, powerful message. It's the answer to the question, "Why should I choose you over everyone else?" And when crafted correctly, it becomes a beacon that draws your ideal clients to you like moths to a flame.

Let's start by diving deep into what makes your business truly unique. This isn't about being different for the sake of being different. It's about identifying the genuine, valuable ways in which your offering stands out. Maybe it's your innovative approach, your unparalleled expertise, or the unique combination of services you provide. Perhaps it's the specific results you consistently deliver, or the distinctive experience clients have when working with you.

Now, here's where many entrepreneurs stumble. They focus solely on what they think makes them great, forgetting to consider what their ideal clients actually care about. Your USP needs to sit at the intersection of what makes you unique and what your ideal clients value most. It's not just about being different; it's about being different in a way that matters to your target market.

To bridge this gap, revisit your ideal client profile. What are their deepest desires? What keeps them up at night? How does your unique offering address these specific needs and wants? Your USP should speak directly to these points, showing your ideal clients that you understand their world and have the perfect solution for their challenges.

Now, let's talk about the art of articulation. A powerful USP is clear, concise, and memorable. It should be something you can comfortably say in one breath, something that sticks in people's minds long after the conversation has ended. Avoid industry jargon or complex language. Instead, use words that resonate emotionally with your ideal clients.

Here's a simple formula to get you started: "We help [ideal client] to [achieve desired outcome] through [your unique method/approach], unlike [common alternatives]." For example, "We help introverted entrepreneurs build six-figure businesses without burning out, through our Quiet Power Method, unlike traditional high-pressure sales techniques."

But don't stop at the first draft. Craft several versions of your USP and test them out. Say them aloud. Share them with trusted colleagues or even some of your ideal clients. Which ones spark interest? Which ones make people lean in and want to know more? Pay attention to the reactions and refine your USP based on this feedback.

Here's a bonus pro tip: Only is better than best. "We're the only X in town who does ABC." Even if X isn't that big a deal, it's still distinctive. Lots of businesses can claim to be the best. The best is subjective. Being the ONLY, isn't.

Remember, your USP isn't just a statement—it's a promise. It sets expectations for what clients can expect when they work with you. Make sure it's something you can consistently deliver on. There's nothing worse than attracting clients with a compelling USP only to disappoint them with the actual experience.

As you integrate your USP into your marketing and communications, be consistent but not repetitive. Your USP should be the thread that runs through all your messaging, but you don't need to recite it word-for-word every time. Instead, let it inform the stories you tell, the benefits you highlight, and the way you describe your services.

Lastly, don't be afraid to refine your USP as your business grows and changes. As you gain new insights into your ideal clients' needs, as you refine your offerings, your USP may need to shift too. This isn't a sign of failure—it's a sign that you're staying responsive to your market and continually improving your value proposition.

Crafting a compelling USP that resonates with your ideal clients is like finding the perfect key for a lock. When you get it right, everything clicks into place. Your marketing becomes more effective, your sales conversations become easier, and your ideal clients start to see you as the obvious choice for their needs. So take the time to craft your USP with care. It's not just a marketing tool—it's the foundation for your business's success in attracting high-quality clients who truly value what you offer.

Articulating Your Value Proposition
Through the Lens of Client Alignment

The essence of articulating your value proposition through the lens of client alignment is showing your potential clients not just what you do, but how perfectly it fits their unique needs, desires, and challenges.

To master this approach, we start with your ideal client's world. What does their day-to-day life look like? What challenges do they face? What goals are they striving towards? This client-centric view is the foundation of a powerful, aligned value proposition.

Now, let's bridge the gap between their world and your offering. How does what you provide solve their specific problems or help them achieve their particular goals? This isn't about generic benefits. It's about painting a vivid picture of how your product or service slots perfectly into their life or business, addressing their unique pain points and amplifying their distinct strengths.

For example, if you're a time management coach for busy entrepreneurs, don't just talk about "increasing productivity." Instead, articulate how your methods will help them reclaim their evenings for family time, reduce the Sunday night anxiety about the week ahead, and free up their time to finally make progress on that passion project they've been putting off. See the difference? You're not just selling time management; you're selling the lifestyle and peace of mind your ideal clients crave.

Language is crucial here. Use words and phrases that your ideal clients use when describing their challenges and aspirations. This creates an immediate sense of "they get me" when they encounter your value proposition. If you're not sure what language to use, go back to your research. Look at how your ideal clients express themselves in forums, social media, or during your conversations with them.

Another powerful technique is to frame your value proposition in terms of transformation. What's the before and after story for your ideal clients? How does their world change when they use your product or service? Be specific and vivid. If you're a web designer for small businesses, don't just say you create beautiful websites. Talk about how your designs turn browsers into buyers, give small business owners the confidence to compete with bigger brands, and become a source of pride and a powerful tool for growth.

Alignment isn't just about what you say, it's also about how you say it. Your tone, your style, the examples you use—all of these should resonate with your ideal clients. If your target market is corporate executives, your language might be more formal and data driven. If you're targeting creative entrepreneurs, a more casual, spirited tone might be appropriate.

Don't be afraid to be specific in your value proposition. Many businesses water down their message in an attempt to appeal to everyone. But remember, when you speak to everyone, you resonate with no one. By articulating a value proposition that's precisely aligned with your ideal clients, you might turn some people off—and that's okay. The goal is to strongly attract the right clients, not to weakly appeal to all.

As you craft your aligned value proposition, consider the objections or hesitations your ideal clients might have. Address these head-on. If you know your ideal clients often worry about the time commitment of implementing new systems, explicitly mention how your solution is designed for busy professionals and can be integrated with minimal disruption.

Lastly, make your value proposition tangible. Use concrete examples, case studies, or even data to illustrate the alignment between what you offer and what your ideal clients need. If you have testimonials from clients who fit your ideal profile, weave these into your value proposition. There's nothing more powerful than having someone who looks just like your ideal client singing your praises.

Articulating your value proposition through the lens of client alignment is like creating a mirror. When your ideal clients encounter it, they should see themselves—their challenges, their aspirations, their unique situation—reflected back at them. But in this reflection, they also see the perfect/ideal solution, the path forward, embodied in what you offer.

This aligned approach transforms your value proposition from a mere description of services into a powerful attractor for your ideal clients. It's not just about what you do; it's about how perfectly what you do fits into their world. Master this, and you'll find your ideal clients are not just interested in what you offer—they'll wonder how they ever managed without you.

Creating Messaging That Naturally Repels Ill-Fitting Clients

Imagine your business as a powerful magnet. But here's the twist—this magnet doesn't just attract; it also repels. And that's a good thing. Creating messaging that naturally repels ill-fitting clients is like fine-tuning your magnet to attract only the metals you want while pushing away the rest. It's a delicate art, but mastering it can transform your business, saving you time, energy, and frustration.

First, let's shift our mindset. The goal isn't to appeal to everyone—it's to deeply resonate with your ideal clients while gently discouraging those who aren't a good fit. This isn't about being exclusionary or rude. It's about being clear, specific, and true to your unique value proposition.

Start by revisiting your ideal client profile and your unique selling proposition. What specific characteristics, values, or needs define your perfect client? Now, consider the flip side. What traits or expectations would make a client a poor fit for your services? This could be anything from budget constraints to communication styles, from project scope preferences to core values.

With these insights in mind, it's time to craft your messaging. The key is to be explicit about who you serve best and why. Don't be afraid to name your ideal client directly in your marketing materials.

For example, if you're a business coach specializing in helping introverted entrepreneurs build sustainable businesses, say so clearly. This automatically signals to extroverted business owners or those looking for aggressive growth strategies that you might not be the best fit for them.

Next, be specific about the problems you solve and the results you deliver. The more precise you are, the more you'll attract ideal clients while naturally filtering out those looking for different outcomes. If you're a web designer who creates minimalist, high-converting sites for tech startups, say that. This naturally repels clients looking for elaborate, design-heavy websites or those in vastly different industries.

Consider using "we're not for you if…" statements. This might feel counterintuitive, but it's incredibly powerful. By explicitly stating who you're not for, you create clarity and save both you and potential clients time and energy. For example, "We're not for you if you're looking for overnight success or quick fixes. Our approach is about sustainable, long-term growth."

Your messaging should also reflect your working style and core values. If you value deep, collaborative relationships with clients, make that clear. This will naturally repel clients looking for a hands-off, do-it-for-me approach. If your process involves intensive strategy sessions before implementation, state that upfront. Clients looking for quick, no-frills solutions will likely look elsewhere.

Pricing can be another effective filter in your messaging. While you don't always need to list exact prices, giving a general range or using phrases like "investment starts at…" can help repel clients whose budgets don't align with your value. Remember, the goal isn't to exclude people based on finances alone, but to signal the level of investment required for the premium results you deliver.

Consider the tone and style of your messaging as well. If your brand personality is bold and no-nonsense, let that shine through. Clients looking for a gentler, more nurturing approach will naturally gravitate elsewhere. Conversely, if your approach is more compassionate and supportive, emphasize that. This will help repel clients expecting a more aggressive, tough-love style.

Case studies and client testimonials can be powerful tools for attracting ideal clients while repelling ill-fitting ones. Choose stories that highlight not just the results you've achieved, but the type of clients you work best with. This gives potential clients a clear picture of whether they align with your ideal client profile.

Repelling ill-fitting clients isn't about being negative or creating barriers. It's about being so clear and specific in your messaging that those who aren't a good fit naturally self-select out. As a result, the clients who do reach out are much more likely to be excellent matches, which saves everyone time and energy.

Lastly, don't be afraid to adapt your messaging over time. As you work with more clients and refine your offerings, you may discover new aspects that define your ideal client or new characteristics that signal a poor fit. Keep refining and adjusting your messaging to stay aligned with your evolving business.

Creating messaging that naturally repels ill-fitting clients is like setting up a filter for your business. It ensures that the clients who come through are more likely to be those you can serve best, leading to better outcomes, happier clients, and a more fulfilling business for you. It's not about shrinking your potential client pool—it's about distilling it to its most potent, aligned form.

Tailoring Your Brand Voice to Attract Your Dream Clients

Your brand voice is more than just the words you use—it's the personality that shines through in all your communications. It's what makes your brand uniquely you, and when aligned correctly, it becomes a powerful magnet for your dream clients. Let's dive into how to craft and refine this voice to confirm it resonates deeply with the exact people you want to attract.

What kind of personality would your ideal client be drawn to? What type of communication style do they respond best to? Are they looking for a bold, challenging authority type? Or do they prefer a nurturing, supportive presence? Understanding this is crucial because your brand voice needs to feel like a natural fit for your dream clients.

Next, consider your own authentic personality and communication style. Your brand voice should be an extension of you or your team—it needs to feel genuine, not forced. The sweet spot is where your natural way of expressing yourself overlaps with what resonates with your ideal clients.

Now, let's get practical. Start by defining three to five key characteristics of your brand voice. These could be adjectives like "bold," "compassionate," "witty," "authoritative," or "down-to-earth." These characteristics will guide all your communications, ensuring consistency across different platforms and touchpoints.

Once you have these characteristics, create a brand voice chart. This chart should include columns for each characteristic, along with dos and don'ts for each. For example, if one of your characteristics is "witty," your dos might include "use clever wordplay" and "reference pop culture," while your don'ts could be "avoid sarcasm" and "never make jokes at a client's expense."

With your brand voice defined, it's time to infuse it into all your communications. This goes beyond just your website copy or social media posts. Your brand voice should be consistent in everything from your email responses to your proposal documents, from your podcast interviews to your client onboarding process.

Your brand voice isn't just about what you say—it's also about how you say it. This includes your sentence structure, the length of your paragraphs, the complexity of your vocabulary, and even your punctuation choices. A bold, energetic brand might use short, punchy sentences with lots of exclamation points. A more academic, authoritative brand might opt for longer, more complex sentences rich with industry-specific terminology.

Don't be afraid to let your personality shine through. If you have a quirky sense of humor that your dream clients appreciate, let it sparkle in your communications. If you're known for your no-nonsense, tell-it-like-it-is approach, make that a cornerstone of your brand voice. Authenticity is key—your dream clients will be drawn to a brand that feels genuine and relatable.

As you implement your brand voice, pay attention to how your dream clients respond. Do certain types of posts or emails get more engagement? Do you notice an increase in inquiries when you lean into a particular aspect of your voice? Use these insights to continually refine and adjust your brand voice.

It's also important to consider the different platforms you're using and how your brand voice might need to be adjusted slightly for each. Your LinkedIn posts might lean more professional, while your Instagram stories could show a more casual, behind-the-scenes side of your brand. The core of your voice should remain consistent, but you can dial certain aspects up or down depending on the platform and context.

One powerful technique is to create a "This, Not That" list for your brand voice. For example, "We're confident, not arrogant," or "We're helpful, not preachy." This helps you and your team understand the nuances of your brand voice and avoid crossing the line into territory that might repel your dream clients.

Lastly, remember that your brand voice should evolve as your business grows and as you gain deeper insights into what resonates with your dream clients. Don't be afraid to experiment and iterate. Your brand voice is a living, breathing aspect of your business—it should grow and mature just as you do.

Tailoring your brand voice to attract your dream clients is like creating a secret handshake between you and your ideal audience. When done right, it creates an instant connection, a feeling of "these are my people" that draws your dream clients in and keeps them engaged. It turns your brand from just another option in a sea of mediocrity into the perfect option, and the only one that's a perfect fit for your dream clients.

Chapter 5:
Medium — Leveraging the Right Channels for Client Attraction

Identifying Where Your Ideal Clients Spend Their Time Online and Offline

The digital world is vast, but your ideal clients aren't everywhere. They have preferred platforms, specific corners of the Internet where they hang out, seek information, and engage with others. Your job is to become a detective and uncover these digital haunts.

Begin with social media. Which platforms do your ideal clients use most? Are they sharing their thoughts on Twitter, networking on LinkedIn, or seeking visual inspiration on Instagram? Don't just guess—dig into the data. Use social listening tools to track mentions of keywords related to your industry. Pay attention to your competitors. Where are they most active and engaging with your target audience.

But don't stop at the obvious platforms. Are there niche forums or online communities where your ideal clients gather? Perhaps there are specific Facebook groups, Reddit communities, or industry-specific platforms where they share challenges, seek advice, and discuss trends. These can be gold mines for understanding your clients' needs and positioning yourself as a valuable resource.

Consider the content your ideal clients consume. Are they avid blog readers, podcast listeners, or YouTube watchers? Do they subscribe to specific industry newsletters or publications? Understanding their content preferences not only tells you where to find them, but also gives you insights into the types of information they value.

Now, let's step away from the screen and into the physical world. Your ideal clients don't just exist online—they have rich, full lives offline too. Where do they go? What events do they attend? Are there specific conferences, workshops, or networking events that attract your target audience?

Think about their daily routines and habits. If you're targeting busy executives, maybe they frequent high-end coffee shops for morning meetings. If your ideal clients are health-conscious entrepreneurs, perhaps they're regulars at local organic markets or yoga studios. Understanding these offline behaviors can open up unique opportunities for connection and visibility.

Don't overlook professional associations or industry groups. These organizations often host events, publish resources, and provide networking opportunities that attract your ideal clients. Becoming a member or partner of these associations can put you directly in the path of your target audience.

As you gather this information, start creating a map of your ideal client's online and offline world. Where do they start their day? How do they seek information when facing a challenge related to your area of expertise? Where do they go to unwind or for professional development?

Quality of presence trumps quantity every time. It's better to be deeply engaged in a few key platforms or communities where your ideal clients are active than to spread yourself too thin trying to maintain a presence everywhere.

Also, consider the different stages of your ideal client's journey. Where do they go when they're just becoming aware of the problem you solve? Where do they turn when they're actively seeking solutions? Your presence and approach might differ depending on where they are in their decision-making process.

Don't forget to validate your findings. Reach out to some of your existing ideal clients or conduct surveys to confirm your assumptions about where they spend their time. You might uncover surprising insights that challenge your initial perceptions.

Lastly, remember that this landscape is always developing. New platforms emerge, preferences shift, and offline behaviors change. Make it a habit to regularly reassess where your ideal clients are spending their time. Stay curious, keep exploring, and be ready to pivot your presence as needed.

By thoroughly identifying where your ideal clients spend their time online and offline, you're setting the stage for meaningful connections. You're positioning yourself to be present in the moments that matter, ready to offer value and build relationships. This targeted approach makes certain that your marketing efforts are focused and effective, allowing you to attract high-quality clients with precision and purpose.

Developing a Multi-Channel Marketing Strategy Aligned with Client Preferences

Not all platforms are created equal in the eyes of your ideal clients. Rank them based on where your clients are most active and engaged. This doesn't mean ignoring less popular channels entirely, but it does mean allocating your resources wisely. Focus on mastering a few key platforms before expanding your reach.

Now, consider the unique strengths of each channel. What type of content performs best on each platform? For instance, LinkedIn might be ideal for sharing in-depth industry insights, while Instagram could be perfect for giving behind-the-scenes glimpses of your work process. YouTube might be your go-to for detailed how-to videos, while your blog serves as a hub for comprehensive guides and case studies.

But here's the key—while your approach may vary across channels, your core message should remain consistent. Think of it as variations on a theme. Your unique value proposition and brand voice should be recognizable whether someone encounters you on social media, your website, or at an in-person event.

Next, let's talk about the customer journey. Different channels often serve different stages of the buyer's journey. For example, social media might be great for awareness and initial engagement, your blog for education and consideration, and email marketing for nurturing leads and driving conversions. Map out how each channel fits into this journey to confirm you're providing the right content at the right stage.

Don't forget about the power of cross-promotion. Each channel should work in concert with the others, creating a seamless experience for your ideal clients. For instance, your podcast might tease exclusive content available on your website, while your email newsletter could highlight your most popular social media posts.

Now, let's address the elephant in the room—content creation. A multi-channel strategy requires a lot of content, and the thought of producing unique pieces for each platform can be overwhelming. Here's where the concept of content atomization comes in handy. Start with a cornerstone piece of content—say, a comprehensive blog post or a detailed video. Then, break this down into smaller pieces tailored for different channels. The key statistics become Twitter posts, the main points transform into an Instagram carousel, and a summary becomes a LinkedIn article.

Each channel should invite interaction with your ideal clients. Ask questions, encourage comments, create polls, and respond promptly to any engagement. This two-way communication is crucial for building relationships and gaining deeper insights into your clients' needs and preferences.

Don't neglect the power of paid advertising in your multi-channel strategy. Platforms like Facebook and LinkedIn offer sophisticated targeting options that allow you to reach your ideal clients with precision. Use these tools to amplify your organic efforts and reach new potential clients who fit your ideal profile.

As you implement your strategy, pay close attention to the data. Use analytics tools to track performance across channels. Which types of content are resonating most? Which channels are driving the most qualified leads? Use these insights to continuously refine your approach, doubling down on what works and adjusting what doesn't.

Lastly, remember that consistency is key. A multi-channel strategy requires commitment and persistence. It's not about making a big splash and then disappearing. It's about showing up consistently, providing value, and gradually building trust and recognition among your ideal clients.

Developing a multi-channel marketing strategy aligned with client preferences is like creating a web of touchpoints that surrounds your ideal clients with value and relevance. When done right, it ensures that no matter where your perfect-fit clients are in their journey, they'll find you ready and waiting with exactly the information, support, or solution they need. This orchestrated approach not only attracts high-quality clients but also positions you as an omnipresent, authoritative figure in your niche.

Mastering Content Creation That Attracts and Pre-Qualifies Ideal Clients

Let's start with the foundation: understanding your ideal client's journey. What questions are they asking at each stage? What information are they seeking? What doubts or objections might they have? Your content should be a roadmap that guides them from their current challenges to the solution you provide, addressing each of these points along the way.

Now, let's talk about the power of specificity. Generic content might cast a wide net, but it rarely catches the exact fish you're after. Instead, create content that speaks directly to your ideal client's specific situation, challenges, and aspirations. Use their language, reference their unique experiences, and address the nuanced problems they face. This level of specificity not only attracts your ideal clients, but also naturally filters out those who aren't the right fit.

Consider creating a content pillars strategy. Identify three to five core themes that align with your expertise and your ideal clients' needs. These pillars will guide your content creation, ensuring you stay focused and relevant. For example, if you're a business coach for creative entrepreneurs, your pillars might include mindset shifts for creatives, pricing strategies for artistic services, and balancing creativity with business acumen.

Now, let's dive into the art of pre-qualification through content. This is about strategically including elements in your content that resonate deeply with your ideal clients while potentially turning away those who aren't a good fit. For instance, if your services are premium-priced, create content that emphasizes the value of investing in quality solutions. This naturally attracts clients who appreciate and are willing to invest in premium offerings while deterring those looking for budget options.

Use storytelling to your advantage. Share case studies and client success stories that mirror the journey of your ideal clients. This not only showcases your expertise but also allows potential clients to see themselves in these stories. If they can't relate to the challenges and aspirations described, it's a clear sign they might not be your ideal client.

Don't shy away from addressing potential objections or concerns in your content. By tackling these head-on, you demonstrate transparency and build trust. It also helps potential clients self-qualify. If your approach or philosophy doesn't resonate with them, they'll likely look elsewhere, saving both of you time and energy.

Consider creating gated content—valuable resources that require users to provide contact information to access. This could be in-depth guides, webinars, or exclusive video series. The topics and positioning of this gated content can act as a powerful pre-qualification tool. Those willing to exchange their information for your insights are demonstrating a higher level of interest and alignment with your offerings.

Don't forget about the power of your unique voice and perspective. Your content should not only inform but also give a taste of what it's like to work with you. Let your personality shine through. Use analogies, examples, or humor that resonates with your ideal clients. This helps attract those who not only need your services but also appreciate your particular style and approach.

As you create content, always keep the next step in mind. What do you want your ideal clients to do after consuming this piece of content? Each piece should have a clear call-to-action that guides interested, qualified prospects to the next stage of their journey with you. This might be signing up for your email list, booking a discovery call, or exploring your services page.

Creating content that attracts and pre-qualifies ideal clients is an ongoing process. Pay attention to the engagement metrics. Which pieces of content are resonating most with your ideal clients? Which are driving the most qualified leads? Use these insights to refine your content strategy over time.

Lastly, don't be afraid to repurpose and repackage your best content. This book is based on my e-course, I've adapted the content in my e-course and transformed it into the book you're reading. Your ideal clients might need to encounter your message multiple times, in different formats, before they're ready to take action. A blog post can become a video, which can be broken down into social media snippets, which can inspire a podcast episode. This multi-format approach confirms you're reaching your ideal clients through their preferred content types.

Mastering content creation that attracts and pre-qualifies ideal clients is like setting up a series of friendly, informative gatekeepers for your business That means by the time a potential client reaches out to you directly, they're already well-informed, excited about your approach, and highly likely to be a great fit. This not only saves you time in the long run, but also sets the stage for more successful, satisfying client relationships.

Utilizing the Alignment Attraction Framework in Networking and Referral Strategies

Let's reframe how we think about networking. It's not about collecting as many contacts as possible; it's about cultivating relationships with the right people. The Alignment Attraction Framework helps you identify who these "right people" are—those who align with your values, complement your services and can help you connect with your ideal clients.

Before you step into any networking situation, whether it's a formal event or a casual coffee meetup, take a moment to center yourself in your alignment. Remind yourself of your unique value proposition, your ideal client profile, and the specific ways you help solve problems. This clarity will act as a filter, helping you gravitate towards the most relevant connections.

Now, let's talk about the art of conversation in networking. Instead of launching into a rehearsed pitch, focus on asking questions that reveal alignment (or misalignment) with your ideal client profile or potential referral partners. For example, "What kind of clients do you love working with the most?" or "What do you find most challenging about your industry right now?" These questions not only show genuine interest but also provide valuable insights into whether this person could be an ideal client or a great referral source.

When you do share about your business, frame it through the lens of the Alignment Attraction Framework. Instead of generic statements, be specific about the unique problems you solve and the particular type of clients you serve best. This specificity acts as a magnet, attracting those who resonate with your approach while gently repelling those who aren't a good fit.

Remember, the goal isn't just to find potential clients; it's also about identifying aligned referral partners. These are professionals who serve the same ideal client profile as you, but in complementary ways. For instance, if you're a business coach specializing in helping introverted entrepreneurs build sustainable businesses, you might align well with a web designer who creates minimalist, high-converting websites for small businesses.

When you find these aligned partners, don't just exchange cards and move on. Explore how you can genuinely support each other. Can you co-create content? Can you refer clients to each other? Can you collaborate on a workshop or webinar? The key is to build relationships based on mutual value and shared ideal client profiles.

Now, let's talk about how to make your current clients your best referral sources using the Alignment Attraction Framework. Start by ensuring your clients deeply understand who your ideal clients are. Share stories of your best client relationships, the specific problems you solve, and the unique way you work. This clarity makes it easier for them to spot potential referrals in their network.

Consider creating a "referral kit" for your best clients and aligned partners. This could include a clear description of your ideal client, common pain points you address, and the unique benefits of working with you. Make it easy for them to make warm introductions by providing email templates or social media posts they can use to make referrals.

Don't forget about the power of strategic partnerships. Look for businesses or professionals who share your values and serve similar client profiles but offer complementary services. For example, if you're a financial advisor for small business owners, you might partner with a small business accountant. Together, you can create a more comprehensive service offering that's incredibly attractive to your shared ideal client base.

When it comes to online networking, apply the same principles of alignment. Be selective about the online communities you join and actively participate in. Look for groups where your ideal clients and aligned partners are likely to gather. When you engage, focus on adding value rather than self-promotion. Share insights, answer questions, and be a helpful resource. This positions you as an expert and naturally attracts aligned connections.

Remember, networking and referrals in the context of the Alignment Attraction Framework are about quality over quantity. It's better to have a smaller network of deeply aligned connections than a vast sea of superficial ones. Nurture these relationships consistently. Share valuable content, make introductions, and always look for ways to support your network.

Lastly, don't underestimate the power of being a connector. When you meet someone who isn't a perfect fit for you but might be ideal for someone in your network, make that introduction. This generosity not only helps others but also reinforces your position as a valuable node in your professional ecosystem.

By utilizing the Alignment Attraction Framework in your networking and referral strategies, you're not just building a network; you're cultivating an ecosystem of mutual growth and success. This approach transforms networking from a sometimes-awkward exchange of business cards into a powerful tool for attracting ideal clients and building meaningful professional relationships.

This ecosystem becomes a self-sustaining entity where aligned individuals naturally support and elevate each other. As you consistently apply the Alignment Attraction Framework, you'll find that your network becomes more than just a list of contacts—it transforms into a community of like-minded professionals who understand and value your unique offerings.

In addition, this aligned network becomes a powerful source of not just referrals, but quality referrals. When your network truly understands your ideal client profile and the specific value you provide, they're able to make targeted, high-quality introductions. This means that the referrals you receive are more likely to be excellent fits for your services, saving you time and energy in the long run.

The Alignment Attraction Framework in networking is about playing the long game. It's not about immediate transactions, but about building lasting relationships that yield benefits for years to come. As you continue to nurture these aligned connections, you'll find that opportunities start to flow more naturally, ideal clients appear more frequently, and your business grows in a way that feels authentic and fulfilling.

In essence, by applying the Alignment Attraction Framework to your networking and referral strategies, you're not just growing your business—you're creating a thriving professional community that supports your success and the success of those around you. This aligned approach ensures that your network becomes one of your most valuable assets, continuously attracting ideal clients and opportunities that are perfectly suited to your unique strengths and offerings.

Chapter 6:
Money — Optimizing Your Business Model for Profitability and Satisfaction

Pricing Strategies That Attract Ideal Clients and Reflect Your True Value

Imagine your pricing as a filter, one that not only makes sure your business thrives but also attracts the clients who truly value what you offer. It's not just about numbers on a page; it's about aligning your worth with the transformative results you deliver. Let's dive into crafting pricing strategies that resonate with your ideal clients and reflect your authentic value.

First, let's shatter a common myth: lower prices do not necessarily attract more clients, especially not the ones you want. In fact, underpricing can often repel your ideal clients, who might associate low prices with low quality or lack of expertise. Remember, your pricing is a statement about your value, your confidence, and the caliber of clients you want to work with.

Start by deeply understanding the value you provide. This goes beyond the immediate deliverables. What's the long-term impact of your work? How does it transform your clients' lives or businesses? Quantify this value where possible. If your service helps businesses increase revenue, gather data on the average growth your clients experience. This concrete evidence of value becomes a powerful tool in justifying your pricing.

Now, consider your ideal client's perspective. What investment level aligns with their expectations of high-quality service? Research what they're currently spending on similar services or alternative solutions. Your pricing should position you as a premium option—not the cheapest, but the best value for the transformative results you deliver.

One powerful strategy is value-based pricing. Instead of basing your rates solely on time or industry standards, price your services based on the value and outcomes you create for clients. This approach often allows you to charge premium rates while still providing excellent value to your clients.

Consider implementing tiered pricing options. This strategy allows you to cater to clients at different levels of readiness or investment capability while still maintaining the integrity of your premium offerings. Your top tier should be priced ambitiously—it's not just about current sales but about shifting perceptions of your value upward over time.

Don't shy away from displaying your prices publicly. Transparency in pricing can act as a pre-qualification tool, attracting clients who are prepared to invest at your level and deterring those who aren't a good fit. If you're concerned about competitors, consider showing price ranges or "starting from" figures.

Package your services in a way that emphasizes value over time or deliverables. Instead of selling "hours" sell outcomes or transformations. For example, rather than offering a "ten-hour consulting package," offer a "Business Transformation Program" that outlines specific results clients can expect.

Consider implementing a "results guarantee" or similar assurance. This not only demonstrates confidence in your abilities but also alleviates potential hesitation from high-value clients. It shows you're invested in their success, not just in making a sale.

Remember, your pricing strategy should be expanded as your business grows and as you gain more evidence of the value you provide. Regularly review and adjust your prices. Many businesses find success with annual or bi-annual price increases, which can be communicated to clients as a natural part of business growth and increased value delivery.

Lastly, don't forget the psychological aspects of pricing. Techniques like charm pricing (ending prices with .99 or .97) or prestige pricing (round numbers for high-end services) can influence perceptions and decisions. Choose the approach that best aligns with your brand and the expectations of your ideal clients.

By crafting pricing strategies that attract ideal clients and reflect your true value, you're not just setting rates—you're positioning your business in the market, communicating your worth, and laying the foundation for rewarding, high-value client relationships. Remember, the right price attracts the right clients. Stand confidently in your value and watch as your ideal clients are drawn to the transformative outcomes you offer.

Implementing the Profit First System
for Financial Stability and Growth

Just as a garden needs the right balance of sunlight, water, and nutrients to flourish, your business requires a robust financial system to grow and prosper. Enter the Profit First system—a game-changing approach that ensures your business isn't just busy, but truly profitable and financially stable.

At its core, the Profit First system flips the traditional accounting formula on its head. Instead of Sales - Expenses = Profit, it advocates for Sales - Profit = Expenses. This simple yet powerful shift prioritizes your profit from the get-go, ensuring that you're building a business that serves you, not just your clients.

Let's break down how to implement this system in your business:

Start by setting up multiple bank accounts. At a minimum, you'll need accounts for:

1. Income

2. Profit

3. Owner's Pay

4. Taxes

5. Operating Expenses

Each time you receive payment, immediately distribute it into these accounts based on predetermined percentages. These percentages will vary depending on your business model and current financial situation, but here's a basic starting point:

- 5 percent to Profit

- 50 percent to Operating Expenses

- 15 percent to Owner's Pay

- 30 percent to Taxes

The magic of this system lies in its simplicity and psychological impact. By physically separating your funds, you create clear boundaries and eliminate the temptation to dip into profits or tax savings for day-to-day expenses.

The Profit account is your business's reward for hard work. It's not just a rainy day fund; it's a celebration of your success. Every quarter, take a distribution from this account as a bonus to yourself or to reinvest in growth opportunities.

The Owner's Pay account guarantees that you, as the business owner, are consistently paid. This regular income creates stability and reinforces the value of your work. Remember, you're not just an employee of your business—you're its most valuable asset.

The Tax account removes the stress of upcoming tax bills. By setting aside money with each payment received, you'll always be prepared for tax time, eliminating last-minute scrambles or unexpected financial hits.

The Operating Expenses account is for the day-to-day running of your business. By limiting this to a specific percentage of income, you're forced to be more intentional and efficient with your spending. This constraint often breeds creativity and innovation in how you operate your business.

Implementing Profit First requires discipline and a shift in mindset. Start by doing a financial health check of your business. What are your current percentages for each category? Don't be discouraged if they're far from the ideal—the goal is progress, not perfection.

Begin with small, manageable changes. If you can't immediately allocate 5 percent to profit, start with 1 percent and gradually increase it. The key is to start the habit of prioritizing profit, even if the amounts are small at first.

Regular review is crucial. Set aside time each month to review your accounts and adjust your percentages if necessary. As your business grows and becomes more efficient, you may be able to increase your profit and owner's pay percentages.

Remember, the Profit First system is flexible. Tailor it to fit your unique business needs. For instance, you might add additional accounts for specific business goals or savings.

One of the most powerful aspects of Profit First is how it changes your approach to expenses. When operating expenses are limited to a specific percentage, you become much more discerning about where you spend money. This often leads to more strategic decisions and can even spark innovation in how you deliver your services.

Implementing Profit First can also positively impact your client relationships. When you're financially stable and confident, it shows in your interactions. You're less likely to take on ill-fitting clients out of financial desperation, and more likely to stand firm on your pricing and policies.

As you grow more comfortable with the system, consider sharing your experience with clients, especially if you work with other business owners. Your success with Profit First can become a powerful testimony to your financial acumen and could even open up new service offerings.

Remember, financial stability isn't just about having more money—it's about creating peace of mind and freedom to focus on what you do best. By implementing the Profit First system, you're not just managing money; you're creating a foundation for sustainable growth and long-term success.

Embracing Profit First is a journey. There will be challenges and adjustments along the way but stick with it. The financial clarity and stability it brings will transform not just your business, but your entire entrepreneurial experience. You'll move from constantly worrying about cash flow to confidently building a profitable, sustainable business that serves both you and your ideal clients.

Developing Packages and Offers
That Resonate with High-Quality Clients

Instead of thinking about what services you can offer, focus on the transformations and outcomes your ideal clients crave. High-quality clients aren't just buying a service; they're investing in a result, a change, a new reality for themselves or their business.

Begin by deeply understanding your ideal client's journey. What is their current pain point? Where do they want to be? Map out the steps between these two points. Your packages should be designed to guide them along this journey, addressing each crucial milestone along the way.

Now, let's talk about the power of tiered offerings. Create a range of packages that cater to different levels of need or commitment. Your entry-level package should offer significant value and solve a specific problem. This acts as a "gateway" for clients to experience your expertise. Your premium packages should offer comprehensive solutions, exclusive benefits, and high-touch service.

When naming your packages, move beyond generic terms like "Basic" or "Premium." Use language that resonates emotionally with your ideal clients and reflects the transformation they'll experience. For instance, a business coach might offer packages like "Clarity Catalyst," "Growth Accelerator," and "Empire Builder."

In crafting your offers, think holistically. What combination of your skills, tools, and methodologies will create the most impactful experience for your clients? Don't just bundle services; create a cohesive journey. Each element should build upon the others, creating a synergistic effect that amplifies the overall value.

Consider incorporating exclusive elements into your higher-tier packages. This could be direct access to you, membership in a mastermind group, or proprietary tools and resources. These exclusive features not only justify premium pricing but also attract clients who value high-level support and are serious about their transformation.

Time frames are crucial for package design. High-quality clients often appreciate structured programs with clear start and end dates. This creates a sense of momentum and achievement. However, also consider offering ongoing support options for clients who want to maintain their results over time.

Don't underestimate the power of storytelling in your package descriptions. Share client success stories that illustrate the journey and outcomes of each package. This helps potential clients envision their own transformation and builds confidence in your ability to deliver results.

Transparency is key for attracting high-quality clients. Clearly outline what's included in each package, the time commitment required, and the expected outcomes. Be specific about the value they're receiving. If possible, quantify the results—whether it's potential time saved, revenue increased, or stress reduced.

Consider creating a signature system or methodology that's unique to your business. This proprietary approach can be a powerful differentiator and can be woven through your package offerings. It gives high-quality clients confidence that they're investing in a proven, specialized solution.

Don't forget about the client experience beyond the core deliverables. How can you make working with you feel special and exclusive? This could include welcome packages, celebration milestones, or unexpected bonuses throughout the journey. These touches elevate the perceived value of your offerings and create memorable experiences that clients rave about.

Pricing your packages requires careful consideration. While we discussed pricing strategies earlier, it's worth noting that your packages should have a clear value ladder. The jump in price between tiers should be justified by a significant increase in value or results.

Remember to build profitability from the start. It's tempting to overdeliver, especially when crafting premium packages, instead, make sure your highest-tier offerings are also your most profitable. This allows you to provide exceptional service without burning out.

Regularly review and refine your packages based on client feedback and results. What elements are clients raving about? Where are they seeing the most significant transformations? Use these insights to continually adapt and improve your offerings.

Lastly, don't be afraid to retire packages that no longer serve your business or attract your ideal clients. As your business grows and evolves, so should your offerings. Regularly assess whether your packages still align with your business goals and the needs of your high-quality clients.

By developing packages and offers that resonate with high-quality clients, you're not just selling services—you're offering transformative experiences. You're creating a clear path for your ideal clients to achieve their deepest desires and most ambitious goals.

Creating a Positive Money Mindset That Supports Client Attraction

Your beliefs about money deeply impact every aspect of your business, from the clients you attract to the value you provide. If you harbor limiting beliefs about money—such as making money is difficult, you don't deserve wealth, or charging premium prices is somehow wrong—these thoughts will subtly sabotage your efforts to attract high-quality clients.

The first step in cultivating a positive money mindset is awareness. I invite you to jot down notes as you reflect on your beliefs about money. What messages did you receive about wealth growing up? How have they developed and changed since then? When you first started your business, how did you decide how much to charge for your services? How has that changed? How do you feel when you think about charging premium prices? Is there any guilt or anxiety associated with financial success? Discovering these underlying beliefs is the first step in transforming them.

Now, let's reframe those beliefs. For every limiting belief you've identified, create a positive, empowering alternative. If you've uncovered a belief like "I don't deserve to charge high prices," reframe it as "My expertise provides immense value, and I deserve to be well-compensated for it." If you believe "There's not enough money to go around," shift to "There are abundant opportunities for financial success in my industry."

Remember, this isn't about positive thinking alone—it's about aligning your mindset with reality. The truth is by attracting ideal clients and providing exceptional value, you're creating a win-win situation. Your financial success enables you to serve at a higher level, create more impact, and ultimately help more people.

One powerful technique for shifting your money mindset is to practice gratitude for your current money and assets. Each day, acknowledge and appreciate the financial reserves you already have, no matter how small. This practice trains your brain to focus on abundance rather than scarcity, creating a positive feedback loop that attracts more financial opportunities.

Another crucial aspect of a positive money mindset is separating your self-worth from your net worth. Your value as a person is not determined by your bank balance or client roster. By internalizing this truth, you free yourself to charge what you're truly worth without fear of rejection or judgment.

Visualization can be a powerful tool in creating a positive money mindset. Imagine yourself easily attracting ideal clients, confidently charging premium prices, and making a significant impact through your work. See yourself handling money with ease and joy. The more vividly you can imagine these scenarios, the harder your subconscious mind will work to make them a reality.

Surround yourself with positive money influences. This might mean reading books about wealth creation, listening to podcasts about the abundance mindset, or joining mastermind groups with entrepreneurs who have healthy relationships with money. The people and information you surround yourself with profoundly impact your mindset.

Practice using empowering language around money. Instead of telling yourself *I can't afford that*, try *How can I create the resources for that*? Instead of *That price is too high*, think *What value would make this investment worthwhile*? This shift in language opens up possibilities and trains your brain to find solutions rather than focus on limitations.

Remember, your relationship with money is mirrored in your clients' experiences with you. When you're confident in your value and comfortable with money, you create a safe space for clients to invest in themselves. Your positive money mindset gives them permission to prioritize their own growth and success.

Don't shy away from celebrating your financial wins, both big and small. Did you sign a new high-ticket client? Hit a revenue milestone? Celebrate it! This reinforces the positive association with money and success in your mind.

As you work on your money mindset, be patient with yourself. Deep-seated beliefs about money often take time to shift. Celebrate your progress, no matter how small, and be compassionate with yourself when old thought patterns resurface.

Importantly, remember that a positive money mindset isn't about greed or accumulating wealth for its own sake. It's about recognizing that financial success enables you to make a bigger impact, serve more people, and create more value in the world. When you prosper, you have more resources to help others and contribute to causes you care about.

Creating a positive money mindset that supports client attraction is an ongoing journey. It's about cultivating a healthy, abundant relationship with money that allows you to show up fully in your business, confidently communicate your value, and attract clients who are excited to invest in the transformation you offer.

As your money mindset shifts, you'll likely notice changes in your business. You might find yourself naturally attracting higher-quality clients, feeling more comfortable stating your prices, and experiencing a greater sense of ease and flow in your financial dealings.

Chapter 7:
Mechanism — Putting the Alignment Attraction Framework Into Action

Developing a Ninety-Day Action Plan for Attracting Ideal Clients

You're about to embark on a ninety-day voyage to the land of ideal clients. Your map is the Alignment Attraction Framework, your compass is your clear vision of success, and your action plan is the detailed route that will get you there. It's time to chart your course and set sail towards a future filled with dream clients and fulfilling work.

Start by setting a clear, measurable goal for the next ninety days. This could be a specific number of new ideal clients, a revenue target, or a combination of both. Make sure this goal is ambitious enough to motivate you, but realistic enough to be achievable in ninety days. Remember, we're looking for progress, not perfection.

Now, break this ninety-day journey into three distinct thirty-day phases. Each phase should have its own focus and set of actionable tasks. This approach allows you to build momentum and adjust your strategy as you go.

Phase 1 (Days one to thirty): Foundation and Preparation

This first month is all about getting your ducks in a row. Tasks might include:

- Refining your ideal client profile using the Alignment Attraction Framework

- Auditing your current marketing materials to confirm they align with this profile

- Creating or updating your core content (website copy, social media bios, pitch deck)

- Identifying the top three platforms where your ideal clients spend their time

- Developing a content calendar focused on topics that resonate with your ideal clients

Phase 2 (Days thirty-one to sixty): Outreach and Engagement

In this phase, you'll start actively reaching out and engaging with potential ideal clients. Activities could include:

- Implementing your content strategy across chosen platforms

- Reaching out to past clients who fit your ideal client profile for testimonials or referrals

- Identifying and joining two to three online communities where your ideal clients gather

- Scheduling coffee chats or discovery calls with potential ideal clients

- Launching a lead magnet specifically designed for your ideal client

Phase 3 (Days sixty-one to ninety): Conversion and Optimization

The final month focuses on turning engagements into clients and refining your approach. Tasks might include:

- Following up with warm leads from your outreach efforts

- Analyzing the performance of your content and adjusting your strategy accordingly

- Requesting and showcasing new testimonials from ideal clients

- Refining your sales process based on feedback and results

- Planning a special offer or event targeted for your ideal clients

Throughout these ninety days, it's crucial to track your progress. Set up a simple system to monitor key metrics like new leads generated, discovery calls booked, and new clients signed. This data will help you understand what's working and what needs adjustment.

Consistency is key. Commit to daily actions that move you closer to your goal. This could be as simple as sharing a valuable piece of content, reaching out to a potential client, or refining your messaging. Small, consistent actions compound over time to create significant results.

Don't forget to build in time for reflection and adjustment. At the end of each thirty-day phase, take a step back and assess your progress. What's working well? What's not resonating? Use these insights to refine your approach for the next phase.

Lastly, celebrate your wins, no matter how small. Landing an ideal client, receiving positive feedback on your content, or even just staying consistent with your plan are all worthy of celebration. These moments of acknowledgment fuel your motivation and reinforce the positive actions you're taking.

By developing and following this ninety-day action plan, you're not leaving the attraction of ideal clients to chance. You're intentionally creating a magnetizing force that draws the right clients to you. Remember, this plan is a living document. Be prepared to adapt and expand as you gain new insights and as market conditions change. Your ability to stay aligned with your ideal clients while remaining flexible in your approach is what will ultimately lead to your success.

As you embark on this ninety-day journey, keep the Alignment Attraction Framework at the forefront of your mind. Let it guide your decisions, shape your messaging, and inform your strategies. With clear goals, a solid plan, and unwavering focus on alignment, you're setting yourself up for a transformative ninety days that will lay the foundation for long-term success in attracting and working with your ideal clients.

Creating Systems and Processes
That Support High-Quality Client Relationships

The power of creating systems and processes that support high-quality client relationships is about building a framework that allows you to show up as your best self for every client, every time.

Let's start with the client journey. Map out every touchpoint a client has with your business, from their first interaction to the completion of your work together and beyond. This might include initial discovery, onboarding, service delivery, feedback collection, and follow-up. For each stage, ask yourself: How can I make this experience not just good, but remarkable for my ideal clients?

Now, let's dive into creating systems for each stage:

1. 1. Initial Contact and Discovery:

Develop a streamlined process for handling inquiries. This could include:

- A well-crafted FAQ page that addresses common questions

- An automated yet personalized response system for initial inquiries

- A structured discovery call process with prepared questions that help you assess client fit

2. Proposal and Contracting:

   Create templates for proposals and contracts that are not only legally sound but also reflect your brand voice and reinforce the value you provide. Consider including:

   - Clear outlines of your process and what clients can expect

   - Testimonials or case studies that demonstrate your impact

   - A simple, streamlined signing process (consider using digital signing tools)

3. Client Onboarding:

   Design an onboarding process that sets the tone for a high-quality relationship:

   - Create a welcome packet that includes all necessary information, forms, and perhaps a small gift

   - Develop a standardized kick-off meeting agenda to make sure that all projects start on the right foot

   - Set up automated reminders for clients to complete necessary pre-work

4. Service Delivery:

    Establish systems that ensure consistent, high-quality service delivery:

    - Create process maps or checklists for each of your core services

    - Develop templates for common documents or deliverables

    - Set up a project management system to track progress and deadlines

5. Communication:

    Implement communication protocols that keep clients informed and engaged:

    - Establish regular check-in schedules (weekly emails, monthly calls, etc.)

    - Create templates for status updates that you can quickly customize

    - Set up a system for clients to easily schedule calls or meetings with you

6. Feedback and Improvement:

    Build in processes for continual improvement:

    - Create a standardized feedback form to send at key milestones and project completion

    - Schedule regular times to review client feedback and implement improvements

    - Develop a system for tracking and celebrating client wins

7. Follow-up and Nurturing:

    Don't let the relationship end when the project does:

    *   Create a follow-up sequence to check in with clients after project completion

    *   Develop a system for staying in touch with past clients (e.g., quarterly value-add emails)

    *   Set up reminders to reach out on important dates (birthdays, business anniversaries)

As you develop these systems, remember that the goal is to create a balance between efficiency and personalization. Your processes should free up your time and mental energy to focus on delivering exceptional value, not create a rigid, impersonal experience.

Leverage technology to support your systems. Customer Relationship Management (CRM) tools, project management software, and automation platforms can be invaluable in streamlining your processes. However, choose tools that align with your work style and your clients' preferences.

Don't forget to document your processes. Develop standard operating procedures (SOPs) for each system. This not only maintains consistency if you're working with a team, but also allows you to easily review and refine your processes over time.

Your systems should reflect your unique approach and brand personality. Infuse your processes with touches that align with your Alignment Attraction Framework. For example, if part of your unique value is deep, personalized attention, ensure your systems allow for and encourage those meaningful interactions.

Regularly audit your systems and processes. Are they truly supporting high-quality client relationships? Are there bottlenecks or pain points that need addressing? Be open to feedback from clients and be willing to make adjustments.

Importantly, communicate your processes to your clients. Let them know what to expect at each stage of working with you. This transparency builds trust and helps manage expectations, both crucial elements of high-quality client relationships.

Lastly, don't let your systems become more important than the relationships they're meant to support. Always be willing to flex and adapt when a situation calls for it. The best systems enhance human interaction, not replace it.

By creating systems and processes that support high-quality client relationships, you're not just improving efficiency—you're crafting a consistently exceptional experience for your ideal clients. This systematic approach certifies that every interaction reinforces your value, strengthens your client relationships, and solidifies your reputation as a premium service provider. With these systems in place, you're free to focus on what you do best: delivering transformative results for your ideal clients.

Measuring and Optimizing Your Client Attraction Efforts

Having clear visibility into what's working, what's not, and how to adjust for maximum impact is critical as you scale your business.

Let's start by identifying the key metrics that matter most for your client attraction efforts. These might include:

1. Lead Generation: How many potential ideal clients are you attracting?

2. Conversion Rate: What percentage of leads turn into paying clients?

3. Client Quality: How well do your new clients align with your ideal client profile?

4. Customer Acquisition Cost (CAC): How much are you spending to acquire each new client?

5. Lifetime Value (LTV) of a Client: What's the total value a client brings over the course of your relationship?

6. Engagement Rates: How are potential clients interacting with your content and communications?

7. Source of Leads: Where are your best leads coming from?

Once you've identified your key metrics, it's time to set up systems to track them consistently. This might involve:

- Using analytics tools for your website and social media platforms

- Setting up tracking links for different marketing campaigns

- Implementing a CRM system to monitor lead progression

- Creating surveys or feedback forms for new clients to assess alignment

Remember, the goal isn't to track every possible metric, but to focus on the ones that provide the most valuable insights for your specific business and goals.

Now, establish a regular rhythm for reviewing these metrics. This could be a weekly check-in on key numbers, a monthly deep dive, and a quarterly comprehensive review. Consistency in reviewing your data is key to spotting trends and making informed decisions.

As you gather data, look for patterns and correlations. Are certain types of content generating more leads? Is there a particular channel that's bringing in higher-quality clients? Do clients from specific sources tend to have a higher lifetime value? These insights will help you focus your efforts where they're most effective.

But numbers alone aren't enough. Combine your quantitative data with qualitative feedback. Regularly talk to your clients about their experience. What attracted them to your services? What almost stopped them from working with you? This firsthand feedback can provide invaluable insights that you might miss if you just rely on numbers.

Now comes the crucial part: optimization. Based on your data and insights, start making strategic adjustments to your client attraction efforts. This might involve:

- Doubling down on content types or topics that resonate most with your ideal clients

- Reallocating resources from low-performing channels to high-performing ones

- Refining your messaging based on what's attracting your best clients

- Adjusting your offer or pricing structure to better align with client needs and values

Adopt a mindset of continuous improvement, always looking for ways to refine and enhance your client attraction efforts.

Don't be afraid to experiment. Set up A/B tests for different aspects of your marketing—try different headlines, call-to-action phrases, or content formats. Let the data guide you in understanding what resonates most with your ideal clients.

As you optimize, keep the Alignment Attraction Framework at the forefront. It's not just about attracting more clients, but about attracting the right clients. Sometimes, a decrease in overall leads can be positive if it means you're more effectively filtering for your ideal clients.

Pay attention to the quality of your client relationships, not just the quantity of new clients. Are your optimization efforts leading to better client experiences? More aligned work? Higher client satisfaction? These factors contribute significantly to long-term success and referrals.

Consider implementing a scoring system for leads based on how well they align with your ideal client profile. This can help you prioritize your efforts and ensure you're focusing on the most promising opportunities.

Remember to look at your metrics holistically. A drop in one area might be offset by improvements in another. For example, you might see fewer leads, but a higher conversion rate and better client quality.

Lastly, celebrate your wins and learn from your setbacks. Every data point, whether positive or negative, is an opportunity to learn and improve. Share these insights with your team or mentor and use them to refine your overall business strategy.

By consistently measuring and optimizing your client attraction efforts, you're not leaving success to chance. You're creating a data-driven, refined approach that becomes more effective over time. This process of continuous improvement confirms that your client attraction efforts become more aligned, more efficient, and more successful with each passing month.

Remember, the goal isn't perfection, but progress. Each optimization, each refinement, brings you closer to a client attraction system that consistently and effortlessly draws your ideal clients to you. With diligent measurement and thoughtful optimization, you're not just hoping for success—you're engineering it, one data point at a time.

Handling Objections and Turning Away Ill -Fitting Clients with Grace

Let's start with handling objections. Remember, objections aren't road-blocks; they're opportunities. They give you insight into your potential client's concerns and a chance to demonstrate your value. Here's how to approach common objections:

1. Price Objections:

    *   Acknowledge the investment required

    *   Refocus the conversation on value and outcomes

    *   Share case studies or testimonials that demonstrate ROI

    *   If appropriate, offer payment plans or different package options

2. Timing Objections:

    *   Explore the reasons behind the timing concern

    *   Highlight the cost of delaying action

    *   If possible, offer a scaled-down starter option

    *   Provide resources they can use in the meantime to start making progress

3. Uncertainty About Fit:

    *   Ask probing questions to understand their specific concerns

    *   Clearly articulate your unique approach and how it addresses their needs

    *   Offer a low-risk way to experience working with you (e.g., a workshop or small project)

Remember, the goal isn't to persuade everyone to work with you. It's to provide clarity and help potential clients make the best decision for their needs.

Now, let's address the delicate art of turning away ill-fitting clients. This can feel counterintuitive, especially when you're trying to grow your business. But remember, saying no to the wrong clients makes room for the right ones. Here's how to do it gracefully:

1. Be Clear and Direct:

    Don't leave room for ambiguity. Clearly state that you don't believe you're the best fit for their needs. For example: "After careful consideration, I don't believe our services are the best match for your current situation."

2. Provide a Brief Explanation:

    Without going into exhaustive detail, offer a concise reason. This could be about specialization, capacity, or alignment of approaches. For instance: "Our expertise is primarily in X, and your needs seem to be more focused on Y."

3. Offer Alternative Resources:

    If possible, provide recommendations for other professionals or resources that might better serve their needs. This shows that you genuinely care about their success, even if you're not the best fit to help.

4. Leave the Door Open (If Appropriate):

    Invite them to reach out in the future. For example: "While we're not the right fit now, if your needs shift towards X in the future, we'd be happy to have another conversation."

5. Express Gratitude:

Thank them for their interest and the time they've invested to explore working with you. This maintains a positive interaction, even if it doesn't result in them becoming a client.

When turning away clients, timing and tone are crucial. Do it as early in the process as possible to avoid wasting their time or getting their hopes up. Maintain a tone that's professional, empathetic, and firm.

Remember, turning away an ill-fitting client isn't a failure—it's a strategic decision that benefits both parties in the long run. An ill-fitting client is likely to be unsatisfied with your services, potentially leading to negative reviews or a damaged reputation.

In some cases, you might encounter pushback when turning a client away. Stay firm but polite. Reiterate your reasons and, if necessary, clearly state that your decision is final. Remember, you're not obligated to work with everyone who wants to hire you.

After turning away a client, take a moment to reflect. Are there patterns in the types of clients you're turning away? This could provide valuable insights for refining your marketing or clarifying your ideal client profile.

Consider creating a standardized process for turning away clients. This could include a template email or script that you can customize for each situation. Having this prepared in advance can make these potentially uncomfortable conversations easier and ensure you maintain a consistent, professional approach.

Remember, your process for turning away clients can impact your reputation. Word-of-mouth is powerful, and even clients you don't work with may talk about their experience with you. By handling these situations with grace and professionalism, you may even turn these interactions into positive referrals.

Lastly, don't forget to acknowledge the emotional aspect of turning away clients. It can be challenging, especially if you're focused on growing your business. Remind yourself that this is a necessary part of building a successful, aligned business. Each time you say no to an ill-fitting client, you're saying yes to creating space for an ideal client.

By mastering the art of handling objections and turning away ill-fitting clients with grace, you're not just maintaining the quality of your client relationships—you're actively shaping the future of your business. You're creating a reputation for integrity, clarity, and high standards that will attract more of your ideal clients in the long run. Remember, every interaction is an opportunity to reinforce your brand and values, even when that interaction doesn't result in a new client. With practice and consistency, these skills will become an integral part of your client attraction strategy, ensuring that your business grows not just in size, but in alignment and satisfaction.

Chapter 8:
Measure — Navigating Your Business with Data-Driven Precision

The Compass of Marketing Measurement:
Guiding Your Business to Success

As small business owners, we often pour our hearts and souls into our marketing efforts. We craft clever social media posts, design eye-catching ads, and network until our voices are hoarse. But without measuring the impact of these efforts, it's like putting messages in bottles, throwing them into the sea, and hoping they reach the right shores. Measurement turns this hopeful guesswork into strategic navigation.

The beauty of measuring your marketing efforts lies in its ability to transform abstract efforts into concrete insights. It's like having a conversation with your market, where every click, every engagement, every sale is your audience speaking back to you. When we take the time to listen to this conversation through data and analytics, we're no longer shouting into the void, hoping someone hears us. Instead, we're engaging in a nuanced dance with our audience, learning their rhythms, understanding their needs, and aligning our steps with theirs.

But where do you start in this vast sea of data? The key is to focus on metrics that truly matter to your business—your Key Performance Indicators (KPIs). These are the North Stars of your measurement efforts, the metrics that directly tie to your business goals and client attraction strategies.

For instance, if your goal is to attract more aligned clients through content marketing, your KPIs might include:

- Engagement rates on your blog posts or social media content

- Click-through rates from your content to your service pages

- Conversion rates of content readers into leads or clients

- Client acquisition cost through content marketing channels

By focusing on these KPIs, you're not just collecting data for the sake of it. You're gathering insights that directly inform your client attraction strategies and business decisions.

The goal of tracking and interpreting your marketing efforts isn't to drown in data, but to gain clarity and direction. Start small, focusing on a few key metrics that align closely with your business goals. As you become more experienced with measuring and interpreting the data, you can expand your analytics toolkit.

One of the most powerful aspects of measuring your marketing efforts is its ability to reveal the true preferences and behaviors of your ideal clients. You might think your audience loves your in-depth technical posts, only to discover through measuring and evaluating the results that it's your personal story-driven content that really resonates and drives engagement. These insights allow you to fine-tune your marketing efforts, creating content and experiences that truly speak to your ideal clients.

Moreover, consistent measuring and analysis allows you to spot trends and patterns over time. You might notice that certain types of content or marketing channels consistently attract more aligned clients. Or you might discover seasonal patterns in your client attraction efforts. These insights enable you to allocate your resources more effectively, doubling down on what works and pivoting away from what doesn't.

But measuring and tracking data isn't just about looking at what's happened in the past. It's about using these insights to chart your course for the future. By understanding which marketing efforts are most effective at attracting aligned clients, you can make data-driven decisions about where to focus your energy and resources moving forward.

As you embrace the compass of measuring marketing efforts, remember that it's an ongoing process. The market is always changing, and so are your clients' needs and preferences. Regular measurement and data analysis allows you to stay agile, adapting your strategies as needed to stay on course towards your business goals.

By making measurement a core part of your marketing strategy, you're not just improving your marketing effectiveness. You're gaining a deeper understanding of your ideal clients, refining your ability to attract them, and ultimately, steering your business towards greater success and fulfillment.

Implementing a Measurement Framework for Client Attraction

The essence of implementing a measurement framework for client attraction is about creating a systematic approach to tracking, analyzing, and optimizing every step of your client's journey, ensuring that each milestone brings them closer to a meaningful engagement with your business.

To begin, let's outline the key stages of client attraction that we need to measure:

1. Awareness: How are potential clients first discovering your business?

2. Engagement: How are they interacting with your content and offerings?

3. Consideration: What steps are they taking to evaluate your services?

4. Conversion: At what point do they decide to become a client?

5. Retention: How long do they remain a client, and what factors influence this?

6. Advocacy: Do they refer others to your business?

For each of these stages, we need to identify specific metrics that provide meaningful insights. Let's break this down:

Awareness Metrics:

- Website traffic sources

- Social media reach and impressions

- Brand mention frequency

Engagement Metrics:

- Content engagement rates (likes, shares, comments)

- Email open and click-through rates

- Time spent on website

Consideration Metrics:

- Downloads of lead magnets or resources

- Attendance at webinars or events

- Requests for more information

Conversion Metrics:

- Lead-to-client conversion rate

- Average time from first contact to becoming a client

- Client acquisition cost

Retention Metrics:

- Client lifetime value

- Repeat purchase rate

- Client satisfaction scores

Advocacy Metrics:

- Net Promoter Score (NPS)

- Number of referrals per client

- User-generated content or testimonials

Now that we've identified what to measure, let's talk about how to implement this framework:

1. Choose Your Tools: Select analytics tools that integrate well with your existing systems. This might include Google Analytics for website data, social media analytics tools, CRM software for tracking client interactions, and survey tools for gathering feedback.

2. Set Up Tracking: Confirm all your digital touchpoints are properly tagged for tracking. This includes installing tracking pixels on your website and setting up event tracking for important actions (like form submissions or resource downloads).

3. Establish Baselines: Before you can improve, you need to know where you're starting from. Gather data for at least a month to establish baseline metrics for each stage of your client attraction process.

4. Set SMART Goals: Based on your baselines, set Specific, Measurable, Achievable, Relevant, and Time-bound (SMART) goals for each stage of the client attraction process. For example, "Increase email newsletter sign-ups by 25 percent in the next quarter."

5. Create a Reporting Dashboard: Develop a centralized dashboard that gives you a quick overview of your key metrics. This could be a spreadsheet, a data visualization tool, or a custom dashboard in your analytics software.

6. Establish a Regular Review Process: Set up weekly, monthly, and quarterly review sessions to analyze your data. Look for trends, identify areas for improvement, and celebrate successes.

7. Test and Optimize: Use your insights to inform A/B tests and optimization efforts. This could involve testing different headlines, call-to-action phrases, or even entire marketing strategies.

8. Close the Loop: Make sure insights from your measurement framework are feeding back into your client attraction strategies. If data shows that a particular type of content is resonating strongly with your ideal clients, create more of it.

As you implement this framework, keep asking yourself: *How can this information help me better serve and attract my ideal clients?*

Also, don't forget the qualitative aspects of measurement. While numbers are important, they don't tell the whole story. Complement your quantitative data with qualitative insights from client feedback, interviews, and your own observations.

Lastly, be patient and persistent. Building a robust measurement framework takes time, and you'll likely need to refine your approach as you go. The key is to start measuring, learn from what the data tells you, and continuously improve your client attraction efforts based on these insights.

By implementing a comprehensive measurement framework for client attraction, you're not just guessing at what works—you're creating a data-driven roadmap for success. This approach allows you to continuously refine your strategies, ensuring that every marketing effort brings you closer to attracting and retaining the clients you love to serve.

Leveraging Data Insights to Refine Your Client Attraction Strategies

In the world of client attraction, your data insights are a litmus test of your client's tastes and interests. Leveraging these insights allows you to transform your client attraction strategies from good to irresistible, serving up exactly what your ideal clients crave.

The first step in this process is to adopt a mindset of curiosity and openness. Your data isn't just a collection of numbers—it's a treasure trove of stories about your clients' behaviors, preferences, and pain points. Approach your data with the enthusiasm of a detective uncovering clues, always asking, *What is this telling me about my ideal clients?*

Start by looking for patterns and trends in your data. Are there certain types of content that consistently generate more engagement? Do specific marketing channels yield higher quality leads? Are there particular times or days when your ideal clients are most responsive? These patterns can provide valuable insights into the habits and preferences of your target audience.

Next, focus on identifying your most effective client attraction strategies. Look at your conversion rates across different marketing channels and tactics. Which ones are not just generating the most leads, but the highest quality leads—those that align most closely with your ideal client profile? This analysis might reveal that while social media brings in a high volume of leads, your email marketing efforts are actually more effective at attracting aligned clients.

Don't just look at what's working—pay equal attention to what's not. Low engagement rates or high bounce rates can be just as informative as high conversion rates. They might indicate that certain aspects of your messaging or offers aren't resonating with your ideal clients. Use these insights to refine or pivot your strategies.

Now, let's talk about segmentation. Your data can help you identify distinct groups within your target audience, each with their own preferences and behaviors. By segmenting your audience based on these insights, you can create more targeted, personalized client attraction strategies. For instance, you might discover that one segment of your audience responds best to in-depth, technical content, while another prefers more visual, story-based messaging.

Use your data to create detailed client journey maps. Where do your ideal clients typically first encounter your brand? What content do they engage with before making a decision? How long is their typical consideration period? Understanding these journeys allows you to optimize each touchpoint, creating a seamless path from initial awareness to becoming a loyal client.

A/B testing is a powerful tool in your data-driven strategy refinement. Use your insights to form hypotheses about what might improve your client attraction efforts, then test these ideas. This could involve testing different headlines, call-to-action phrases, or even entire marketing approaches. Let the data guide you in determining which variations are most effective for attracting your ideal clients.

Don't forget to look at the bigger picture. While it's important to analyze individual metrics, also consider how different data points interact. For example, you might notice that while a particular marketing campaign didn't directly lead to many new clients, it significantly increased brand awareness, which in turn led to more inbound inquiries over time.

As you refine your strategies based on data insights, always keep your ideal client profile in mind. It's easy to get caught up in improving metrics for their own sake, but the ultimate goal is to attract more aligned clients. Ask yourself, *Are these changes helping me connect more effectively with the clients I truly want to serve?*

Remember that data-driven refinement is an ongoing process. Set up regular review periods to analyze your data, draw insights, and make strategic adjustments. This might be monthly for minor tweaks and quarterly for larger strategic shifts.

Importantly, don't let data paralysis set in. While it's crucial to base your decisions on data, don't get so caught up in analysis that you fail to take action. Use your insights to inform your decisions, but also trust your intuition and expertise about your business and clients.

Lastly, share your data insights with your team. This not only helps everyone understand the rationale behind strategic changes but also encourages a culture of data-driven decision-making throughout your organization.

By leveraging data insights to refine your client attraction strategies, you're not just improving your marketing effectiveness—you're continuously aligning your business more closely with the needs and preferences of your ideal clients. This iterative, data-driven approach ensures that your client attraction efforts become more targeted, more effective, and more aligned over time.

Remember, the goal isn't perfection but continuous improvement. Each refinement, each optimization based on your data insights, brings you one step closer to a client attraction strategy that resonates deeply with your ideal clients.

Creating a Culture of Measurement and Continuous Improvement

To begin cultivating a great company culture, start with yourself. As the leader of your business, your attitude towards measurement and improvement sets the tone for your entire team. Embrace a growth mindset, viewing challenges and setbacks not as failures, but as valuable learning opportunities. Share your own data-driven insights and decision-making processes with your team, demonstrating the value of this approach in action.

Next, make data accessible and understandable to everyone in your organization. Create dashboards or regular reports that clearly communicate key metrics related to client attraction and satisfaction. But don't just share numbers—provide context and encourage discussion about what these metrics mean for your business and your clients.

Encourage curiosity and questioning. Create an environment where team members feel safe asking "why" and challenging assumptions. This could involve regular brainstorming sessions where you analyze data, evaluate progress towards goals, and explore potential improvements to your client attraction strategies.

Implement a system for collecting and acting on ideas from all levels of your organization. Your team members who interact directly with clients often have valuable insights that may not be captured in quantitative data. Create channels for them to share these observations and incorporate them into your improvement efforts.

Make learning a core part of your business culture. This could involve setting aside time for team members to explore new analytics tools, attend webinars on data-driven marketing, or share insights from industry reports. Consider creating a knowledge-sharing platform where team members can post interesting articles, case studies, or their own data-driven discoveries.

Align your recognition and reward systems with this culture of measurement and improvement. Celebrate not just achievements, but also valuable learnings and innovative ideas for improvement. This reinforces the idea that gathering insights and striving for continuous improvement are valued just as much as hitting targets.

Incorporate data analysis and improvement planning into your regular meeting rhythms. This could involve weekly team huddles to review key metrics, monthly deep dives into specific areas of your client attraction strategy, and quarterly strategic planning sessions based on accumulated insights.

Don't just focus on quantitative data. Encourage qualitative feedback as well, both from clients and team members. Regular surveys, feedback sessions, and open discussions can provide valuable context to your quantitative metrics and uncover insights that numbers alone might miss.

Create a system for turning insights into action. It's not enough to gather and analyze data—you need a clear process for implementing improvements based on your findings. This could involve creating improvement task forces, assigning specific team members to champion certain metrics, or incorporating data-driven goals into your project management system.

Building culture takes time and patience. It's about gradual, consistent change rather than overnight transformation. Celebrate small wins and learnings along the way, reinforcing the value of this approach with each success story.

Be open to experimenting with different measurement tools and techniques. As your business evolves, refine and update your measurement practices. Encourage team members to explore and suggest new ways of gathering and analyzing data that might provide fresh insights into your client attraction efforts.

Importantly, see to it that this culture of measurement and improvement always stays connected to your core mission and values. The ultimate goal isn't just to improve metrics, but to better serve your ideal clients and fulfill your business purpose. Regularly revisit your mission and values, ensuring that your measurement and improvement efforts are aligned with these fundamental guideposts.

Lastly, lead by example by being open to feedback and change. Show your team that you're willing to adjust your own strategies and approaches based on data and insights. This vulnerability and adaptability from leadership can be a powerful catalyst for fostering a truly data-driven, improvement-focused culture throughout your organization.

By creating a culture of measurement and continuous improvement, you're not just optimizing your client attraction strategies—you're building a resilient, adaptive business that can thrive in any market conditions. This culture becomes a competitive advantage, allowing you to consistently refine your approach, stay aligned with your ideal clients' needs, and continuously enhance the value you provide.

Remember, this culture isn't about perfection—it's about progress. It's about fostering an environment where every team member is empowered to contribute to the ongoing evolution and success of your business.

Chapter 9:
Maintenance — Sustain Your Success with the Alignment Attraction Framework

Congratulations! You've journeyed through the transformative process of mastering the Alignment Attraction Framework and you're ready to Get More Clients You Love!. You've delved deep into understanding your ideal clients, crafted compelling messages that resonate with them, leveraged the right channels to reach them, and optimized your business model to serve them best. But remember, this is not the end—it's just the beginning of a new chapter in your business journey.

As you move forward, keep the Alignment Attraction Framework at the core of your business strategy. This framework isn't a onetime implementation; it's a dynamic, adaptable approach that grows with you and your business. Here are some key points to remember as you continue to attract and serve the clients you love:

1. Continual Refinement:

    Your understanding of your ideal client will deepen over time. Stay curious and open to new insights. Regularly revisit your ideal client profile and refine it based on your experiences and the evolving market landscape.

2. Consistency Is Key:

The power of the Alignment Attraction Framework lies in its consistent application across all aspects of your business. From your marketing messages to your service delivery, confirm that everything aligns with your ideal client profile and core values.

3. Embrace Feedback:

Your clients are a gold mine of insights. Regularly seek feedback, not just on your services, but on their entire experience with your business. Use this information to fine-tune your approach and strengthen your alignment.

4. Stay Adaptable:

Markets change, client needs expand, and new opportunities emerge. While staying true to your core values and ideal client profile, be prepared to adapt your strategies and offerings as necessary.

5. Adjust Your Mindset:

Remember, attracting ideal clients starts with your mindset. Regularly check in with your beliefs about money, success, and your own worth. Address any limiting beliefs that may be holding you back from fully embracing your value.

6. Celebrate Your Successes:

Take time to acknowledge and celebrate your wins, both big and small. Each ideal client you attract, each successful project you complete, is a testament to the power of alignment in your business.

7. Community and Support:

Consider joining or creating a community of like-minded entrepreneurs who are also committed to serving clients they love. This support network can provide encouragement, accountability, and valuable insights as you continue to grow.

8. Continuous Learning:

The business landscape is always evolving. Stay committed to your own growth and learning. Attend workshops, read widely, and consider working with mentors who can provide fresh perspectives and challenge you to reach new heights.

9. Trust the Process:

There may be times when progress feels slow, or you face setbacks. Trust in the Alignment Attraction Framework and the foundations you've built. Remember, aligned success is not just about quick wins, but about building a sustainable, fulfilling business.

10. Pay It Forward:

As you experience success with this framework, consider how you can share your knowledge and experiences with others. Whether through mentoring, creating content, or simply sharing insights with your network, your journey can inspire and guide others on their path to alignment.

Chapter 10:
Mastermind — The Bonus "M" and My Secret Weapon

A s I reflect on the journey we've shared through this book, I can't help but smile. We've covered a lot of ground, haven't we? From attracting the right clients to building a business that aligns with your values, we've explored strategies that can transform not just your business, but your life. But I've saved the best for last. I want to tell you about my secret weapon, the tool that has been more valuable to me than any business strategy or marketing tactic. I'm talking about my Mastermind group.

Now, you might be thinking, *Mastermind groups? Aren't those just for Fortune 500 CEOs or Silicon Valley startups*? Let me assure you, they're not. In fact, Masterminds are a powerful tool for businesses of all sizes, from solopreneurs to large corporations. For me, the experience has been nothing short of transformational.

My Mastermind journey began in an unexpected place. It grew out of a business connections group—though the founder would bristle at calling it a "networking group." In honor of her memory, I'll refrain from using that term. At the time, the only thing the members of our group had in common was that we were working for ourselves or someone else and shared a desire to connect. We all happened to live in the same general area, which was the only true criterion. Simple beginnings, right?

We started with nine members and a structured agenda. But what it has become is something so meaningful to me that it has become an integral part of my process—perhaps the most important part.

As many of you know from your own experience, being a business owner is lonely, even if you have a partner. Your non-business owner friends don't understand. Your family, as much as they love and support you, often can't relate to the unique challenges you face. That's where the Mastermind comes in.

Over time, our group naturally distilled down to four people. Four women, Carolina, Hannah, Lindsey, and me, to be precise. We come from different backgrounds, are at different stages of life, and have vastly different experiences. We share a powerful purpose: to speak from the heart, to be vulnerable, to be open, to be loving, and to be supportive and challenging all at the same time.

In our meetings, there's no room for pretense or facade. We've created a space where we can lay our struggles bare, celebrate our victories (no matter how small), and work through our challenges together. It's a place where we can admit our fears, our doubts, and yes, even our failures.

I remember one meeting where I confessed that I was still struggling with a particular client issue—one that I thought I had resolved months ago. Instead of judgment, I was met with understanding nods and gentle questions that helped me see the problem from a new angle. That's the beauty of a Mastermind; it's a group of people who are willing to let you make the same mistake over and over but will call you on it in the gentlest way.

These women have helped me rebuild not just my business, but my life, and my soul. They've been there through the tough decisions, the sleepless nights, and the moments of triumph. They've challenged my thinking, pushed me out of my comfort zone, and celebrated my successes as if they were their own.

So, if there's one piece of advice I can leave you with, it's this: find your Mastermind. Find a group of people who you can lean into, trust, feel supported by, and won't be judged. If you don't currently have a network like this, create one. Reach out to other business owners in your area or connect with like-minded individuals online. Start small, be patient, and let the group evolve naturally.

I know it might seem daunting. You might be thinking, *But I'm not ready. My business isn't successful enough. I don't have anything to offer*. Let me stop you right there. Your experiences, your challenges, your perspective—these are all valuable. You have something unique to bring to the table, and you'll be surprised at how much you can help others even as they're helping you.

A Mastermind is more than just a business tool. It's a lifeline. It's a support system. It's a brain trust. It's a cheering squad. It's a safe space to be vulnerable and a launching pad for your greatest ideas. It's all of these things and more. Because at the end of the day, success is sweeter when shared, challenges are easier when you have support to get through them, and the journey is far more enjoyable with friends by your side.

Remember, the ultimate goal of the Alignment Attraction Framework is not just to get more clients—it's to create a business that truly resonates with who you are and the impact you want to make in the world. It's about building relationships with clients who value your unique gifts and approach, and who inspire you to do your best work.

Thank you for giving me the opportunity to share what I've learned by developing and implementing this framework. If you've ever found yourself in a proverbial, or literal, parking lot wishing for a better way to attract what you want, please trust that what you've just read was not hyperbolic. That frustration is real, but so is a better path forward. Carry with you the knowledge that you have the power to shape your business destiny. You're not at the mercy of the market or fleeting trends. With the Alignment Attraction Framework as your guide, you have the tools to consistently attract and serve clients you love, creating a business that's not just profitable but deeply fulfilling.

So, go forth. Build your business. Believe in your abilities and talents. Attract those dream clients. And never underestimate the power of a strong Mastermind.

Made in the USA
Columbia, SC
07 December 2024